Airplanes and Helicopters
of the U.S. Navy

Left: Early A-7B Corsair. *Below:* A UH-46 Sea Knight delivers supplies to a ship at sea.

Airplanes and Helicopters
of the U.S. Navy

FRANK J. DELEAR

ILLUSTRATED WITH PHOTOGRAPHS

DODD, MEAD & COMPANY · NEW YORK

To the Twelve O'Clock Scholars of Cape Cod

PICTURE CREDITS

Beech Aircraft Corporation, 89, 114, 116; Bell Helicopter Company, 34, 102, 103, 130, 131, 132; Boeing photo, 18; Douglas Aircraft Company, 54, 56, 106, 129; Grumman Aerospace Corporation, 37, 38, 39, 52, 53, 60, 91, 92, 93, 94, 139; Herreshoff Manufacturing Co., 10; Kaman Aerospace Corporation, 80, 111; Conrad Larson Collection, 19, 32 (bottom); Lockheed Aircraft, 35; Lockheed-California Company, 86, 87; Lockheed-Georgia Company, 95; McDonnell Aircraft Company, 40, 41, 42, 43, 44, 45, 46; McDonnell Douglas Corporation, 135; Naval Photographic Center, 15, 28; North American Rockwell, 118, 119, 121, 122, 123; Pratt & Whitney Aircraft, 24 (bottom), 25; Sikorsky Aircraft, 66, 77, 108, 112, 136, 137; U.S. Naval Historical Center, 14; U.S. Navy photo, 12, 13, 17, 24 (top), 26, 29, 31, 63, 79; U.S. Navy-Boeing-Vertol, 2 (bottom), 99, 100; U.S. Navy-Grumman Aerospace Corporation, 58; U.S. Navy-Kaman Aerospace Corporation, 81; U.S. Navy-Lockheed-California Company, 73, 74; U.S. Navy-Lockheed-Georgia Company, 96, 97; U.S. Navy-Rockwell International Corporation, 71; U.S. Navy-Sikorsky Aircraft, 83, 85; U.S. Navy-Vought Corporation, 2 (top), 48, 49, 50, 69; United Technologies Archives, 20, 21, 22, 23, 27, 30, 32 (top), 33, 105; Vought Corporation, 125, 126, 127.

1 2 3 4 5 6 7 8 9 10

Library of Congress Cataloging in Publication Data

Delear, Frank J.
    Airplanes and helicopters of the U.S. Navy.

    Includes index.
    1. Airplanes, Military—United States. 2. Military helicopters—United States. 3. United States. Navy—Aviation. I. Title.
UG1243.D43   358.4′183′0973   81-15259
ISBN 0-396-08031-6   AACR2

Acknowledgments

Especially helpful in providing source material for this book were William J. Armstrong, historian, Naval Air Systems Command; Harvey Lippincott and Beatrice LaFlamme of United Technologies Archive & Historical Research Center; Robert O. Anthony, archivist, Yale University Library; Sylvester Gookin, boating and yachting historian, Marshfield, Massachusetts; Gordon Nelson, aviation historian, Squantum, Massachusetts; and Ralph Lightfoot, aeronautical engineering consultant, Chatham, Massachusetts.

Helpful also, in specialized areas, were two former Naval aviators, Mike Baxter of Sikorsky Aircraft, and Conrad Larson, Peterborough, New Hampshire; David R. Smith, Airship International Press; C. R. Haberlein, Naval Historical Center; Desdie Prince, Legislative and Information Office, Naval Air Systems Command; Robert A. Carlisle, Photojournalism Branch, Navy Office of Information; J. L. Evans, Fleet Air Reconnaissance Squadron 4, Patuxent River, Maryland; and Arthur L. Schoeni, Dallas, Texas.

My appreciation to the following representatives of the aircraft industry: Don Fertman, Sikorsky Aircraft; Frank Pedroja, Beech Aircraft Corporation; Allen Cobrin, Grumman Corporation; Martin Reisch, Bell Helicopter Textron; Eldon Corkill and Mike Hatfield, Vought Corporation; Joseph Dabney, Lockheed-Georgia Company; Craig Smith and Doree Martin, McDonnell Aircraft Company; Dent Williams, Rockwell International Corporation; Gordon Williams, Boeing Airplane Company; Bruce Goulding, Kaman Aerospace Corporation; Kristin Lane, Grumman Aerospace Corporation; James Ragsdale and Joanne Bergener, Lockheed-California Company; David Eastman, Douglas Aircraft Company; and Madelyn Bush, Boeing Vertol Company.

BOOKS BY FRANK J. DELEAR

FAMOUS FIRST FLIGHTS ACROSS THE ATLANTIC

IGOR SIKORSKY: HIS THREE CAREERS IN AVIATION

HELICOPTERS AND AIRPLANES OF THE U.S. ARMY

THE NEW WORLD OF HELICOPTERS

CONTENTS

Preface/FROM SEA TO AIR   9

Part One/A STORY OF ACHIEVEMENT   11

Part Two/FIGHTER AIRCRAFT   37
    Grumman F-14 Tomcat   37
    McDonnell Douglas F-4 Phantom II   40
    McDonnell Douglas F-18 Hornet   44

Part Three/ATTACK AIRCRAFT   48
    Vought A-7E Corsair II   48
    Grumman A-6E Intruder   51
    Douglas A-3D Skywarrior   54
    Douglas A-4 Skyhawk   56

Part Four/RECONNAISSANCE AIRCRAFT   58
    Grumman EA-6B Prowler   58
    Grumman E-2C Hawkeye   61
    Lockheed EC-130Q Hercules   63
    Sikorsky RH-53D Sea Stallion   65
    Vought RF-8G Crusader   68
    North American RA-5C Vigilante   70

Part Five/SEARCH AIRCRAFT   73
    Lockheed S-3A Viking   73
    Sikorsky SH-3 Sea King   76
    Kaman SH-2 Seasprite   80
    Sikorsky SH-60B Seahawk   83

Part Six/PATROL AIRCRAFT   86
    Lockheed P-3 Orion   86

Part Seven/TRANSPORT AIRCRAFT   89
    Beechcraft UC-12B   89
    Grumman C-2A Greyhound   91
    Grumman C-1A Trader   93
    Lockheed C-130 Hercules   95
    Boeing Vertol H-46 Sea Knight   98
    Bell UH-1 Iroquois   102
    McDonnell Douglas C-9B Skytrain II 105
    Sikorsky CH-53E Super Stallion   107

Part Eight/RESCUE AIRCRAFT   110
    Kaman HH-2 Seasprite   110

Sikorsky HH-3A Sea King   111

Boeing Vertol HH-46A Sea Knight   112

Bell HH-1K Iroquois   113

Part Nine/TRAINER AIRCRAFT   114

Beechcraft T-34 Mentor   114

Beechcraft T-44A King Air   116

Rockwell International T-2 Buckeye   118

North American T-28 Trojan   121

North American T-39 Sabreliner   123

Vought TA-7C Corsair II   125

Douglas TA-4 Skyhawk   128

Bell TH-57A Sea Ranger   130

Bell TH-1L Iroquois   131

Grumman TE-2C Hawkeye   133

Part Ten/THE FUTURE   134

Index   141

Preface / FROM SEA TO AIR

In Jules Verne's 1904 book, *Master of the World*, the fictional ship *Terror* could travel under the sea, on it, on land, and in the air, all at incredible speeds. A fantasy, but one which contained a great truth: nations whose navies controlled the seas were, in fact, "masters of the world."

Later, man learned to sail still another "sea," the vast ocean of air which envelops the globe and through which he can speed anywhere on earth. Today's U.S. Naval aircraft are the winged ships designed to help rule the seas by first controlling the air above.

The age-old art of shipbuilding made many contributions to the twentieth-century science of aeronautics. In the design of the swift torpedo boats of the nineteenth century, for example, the search was for the best combination of low resistance (drag), strong structure, and light weight. To achieve those goals the torpedo boat builders developed their own technology and employed the best artisans of their day.

At the turn of the century the racing yacht *Constitution*, then being built by Captain Nathanael Herreshoff at his shipyard in Bristol, Rhode Island, introduced a system of ship construction now used all over the world. Known as the Isherwood system, it consists of longitudinal beams held in place by deep web frames, or ribs—the lightest known system of framing and one which for many years has been used for both ships and aircraft.

Herreshoff also devised instruments for testing the rigging and materials of his racing yachts while the vessels were under full sail. The devices were forerunners of the strain gauges that appeared in the aircraft industry about twenty years later.

The science of aerodynamics, especially at high speeds, is closely related to hydrodynamics. Today's wind tunnels are the aircraft industry's counterparts of shipbuilders' towing tanks in which model ship hulls were first tested more than two hundred years ago. Tapered "lee-boards," used for three hundred years on the shallow-draft fishing boats on the waters of Holland's Zuider Zee to prevent the boats from sliding sideways, bear an uncanny resemblance to airplane wings (or airfoils), both in appearance and function.

Powered ships and aircraft alike are propelled by forces produced by propellers or by revolving turbine blades. The rudders of ships and the aft control surfaces of submarines and torpedoes are virtually identical with the tail assemblies of airplanes and dirigibles. The planes on the bows of modern subs have their counterparts on supersonic jets. Dirigibles were similar in shape to submarines, while the use of ballast for changing depth (altitude) added further to the kinship between subs and lighter-than-air ships.

The Burgess Company of Marblehead, Massachusetts, a well-known boat builder, produced seaplanes and flying boats for the U.S. Navy between 1912 and 1917. Later the Navy employed shipbuilders to construct the wood hulls for its huge NC flying boats used in 1919 in a pioneering attempt to fly the Atlantic. (Herreshoff built the hull for the NC-4, the only one of the planes to complete the flight successfully, the first air crossing of the Atlantic.)

Much more could be said about the historic ties between ships of the sea and ships of the air as seen in the similarities embodied in the endless search for the most efficient movement of vehicles through water and air. Next, a brief look at the accomplishments of U.S. Naval Aviation from its beginnings to the present.

Needlelike lines of the U.S. Navy's U.S.S. *Cushing*, a 140-foot torpedo boat built in 1890 by N. G. Herreshoff, were forerunners of today's slim supersonic aircraft.

Part One / A STORY OF ACHIEVEMENT

Why Naval Aviation? In the words of William J. Armstrong, historian for the Naval Air Systems Command, Washington, D.C., "From 1911 to the present the main goal of Naval Aviation has been not so much to build an air force as to increase the operational effectiveness of the Navy."

From the beginning, Armstrong points out, those who envisioned the use of aircraft by the Navy stressed the need for sea-going aircraft rather than flying machines tied to land bases. As a result, Naval aircraft went to sea, serving both to defend the fleet and to increase the range of Naval operations. With aviation the Navy can bring a powerful force to bear against an enemy on, under, or above the sea, and even upon land. Increasingly, aircraft have given the Navy a level of strength impossible without them.

Over the years, spanning more than seven decades, the Navy has used all the basic types of aircraft. Included have been airplanes (both land- and carrier-based, seaplanes, and flying boats), lighter-than-air craft (blimps and huge dirigibles), and helicopters (whose unique qualities have apparently ended forever the need for blimps and ship-based seaplanes).

Naval Aviation, rich in tradition and achievement, traces its beginnings back to 1898 when action by the then Assistant Secretary of the Navy, Theodore Roosevelt, led to formation of a committee to study the application of aviation to the military. The Navy decided that such an apparatus as a flying machine "pertains to land service and not to the Navy"—understandable, considering that the airplane had yet to be invented.

Eventually, though, the Wright brothers' flights in 1903, and further aeronautical progress, forced the Navy to appoint an officer to handle queries about aviation matters. Captain Washington Irving Chambers, assistant to the Secretary of the Navy's Aide for Material, was given the task. He performed it nobly, almost single-handedly keeping Naval Aviation alive during its infant years.

In the fall of 1910 Chambers arranged for a civilian pilot, Eugene Ely, to try a flight from a Naval vessel. Ely made the takeoff on November 14, flying a Curtiss biplane from an 83-foot platform on the bow of the cruiser *Birmingham*, anchored in Hampton Roads, Virginia, and landing five minutes later on nearby Willoughby Spit. It was the first flight from a Naval surface vessel. On January 18, 1911, Ely reversed the trip by landing his plane on a 120-foot platform built on the stern of the U.S.S. *Pennsylvania*, anchored in San Francisco Bay—the first landing on a Naval vessel.

The next few years found Chambers and other pioneers fighting the apathy and even hostility of tradition-bound older officers in order to get their new ideas accepted. Progress was slow but steady. Among the highlights:

• December, 1910—Chambers sends Lieutenant Theodore G. Ellyson to the Glenn H. Curtiss aviation camp at North Island, San Diego, California, where Ellyson becomes the first U.S. Navy man to qualify as a Naval aviator.

• January 29, 1911—Curtiss flies his new "hydroaeroplane" (or hydroplane) near North Island, the first plane to take off from water. Later he taxies the plane alongside the cruiser *Pennsylvania* where the craft is hoisted aboard and off again by the ship's crane.

First flight from a Naval vessel: Eugene Ely, in a Curtiss biplane, November 14, 1910, from cruiser *Birmingham*.

12

U.S. Navy's first airplane, Curtiss A-1 Triad, shown as a landplane, 1911.

● March 4, 1911—The Navy appropriates $25,000 to develop "aviation for Naval purposes," and in July accepts its first aircraft, the Curtiss A-1 Triad, so-named because of its ability to operate from land, water, and in the air. The A-1 was built at the Curtiss plant in Hammondsport, on Lake Keuka, New York.

● Fall, 1911—The Navy acquires its first engineering test pilot, Holden C. Richardson, whose first job is redesign of a catapult developed by Chambers. Result: the new Curtiss A-3 hydroplane is launched by catapult from a barge on November 12, 1912, the first successful launching of a plane by catapult.

● Spring, 1913—In an expansion move, the Navy schedules 12 officers for flight training; by fall, 34 applications for aviation duty are on file; at year's end Naval Aviation consists of six pilots on flight status and six airplanes.

● January, 1914—Old Navy Yard at Pensacola, Florida, becomes site of the first U.S. Naval Air Station, offering a warm climate and a stretch of sandy beach. Under command of Lieutenant-Commander Henry C. Mustin, the beach is cleared of hurricane debris, tent hangars erected, and wood ramps built to the water. A flying school is set up there with Lieutenant John H. Towers in charge.

Early seaplanes and tent hangars on the beach at the first Naval Air Station, Pensacola, Florida, in 1914.

• March, 1915—Improved flight pay, doubled pensions, and benefits for crewmen killed or disabled in Naval Aviation are approved.

• July, 1916—The first catapult launching from an American vessel underway is made from the stern of the cruiser *North Carolina* in Pensacola Bay by a Curtiss AB-3 flying boat flown by Lieutenant Godfrey deC. Chevalier.

• October, 1916—Orders are placed for 25 N-9s, the most successful of the early Curtiss line of trainers and the first built for the Navy with controls connected as in modern airplanes; also the first delivered with safety belts installed.

Other progress came during those years—the first night flights, first use of radio in an airplane, establishment of "aeronautical corps" in each State Naval Militia, first steps toward mobilizing science to help the Navy meet new conditions of warfare, successful experiments with aerial cameras, and the beginnings of the Navy's Aeronautical Engine Laboratory at the Washington, D.C., Navy Yard.

Despite progress, U.S. Naval Aviation was ill-equipped for World War I. When the United States entered that war on April 6, 1917, its Naval aircraft consisted of 45 seaplanes, six flying boats, three landplanes, and one blimp—none of them ready for combat. By Armistice Day, November 11, 1918, this meager force had grown to 695 seaplanes, 1,170 flying boats, 242 landplanes, and 15 blimps.

During those nineteen months manpower rose from 43 Naval aviators (including five Marines) and 239 enlisted men to 6,716 officers and 30,683 enlisted men in Naval units, plus 282 officers and 2,180 men

Single-engine Curtiss HS flying boats at U.S. Naval Air Station, Brest, France, in World War I.

in Marine Corps units. At the Armistice the number of U.S. Naval bases had grown from one (Pensacola) to 39, including 27 overseas, chiefly to support the flying boats.

Technically the top Naval air development of World War I was the long-range flying boat as seen in the twin-engine Curtiss H-12 and H-16 and the single-engine HS. Overseas, U.S. Navy crews flew the HS and H-16 types when these American-built craft became available in 1918, but before that used French-, British-, and Italian-built planes. Their duties included antisubmarine patrols, convoy escort, and bombing German U-boat pens and other military targets.

The H-16s were built not only by Curtiss but also at the new Naval Aircraft Factory (NAF) opened in 1917 in Philadelphia. (The NAF, with most of its production concentrated during World Wars I and II, built almost 2,000 planes, including both Navy-designed and industry-designed aircraft, before its manufacturing ended in 1945.)

No name is more prominent in the early days of Naval Aviation than Curtiss and some have even called Glenn Curtiss "the father of Naval Aviation." Curtiss flew the first airplane off water, met the Navy's strict requirements for a practical seaplane, built the first plane to land on and take off from a ship (feats performed by a Curtiss-trained flier, Ely), and built the Navy's first operational aircraft and many hundreds more. The Navy's first aviation mechanics learned their trade under Curtiss' instruction. His flying boat *America* (1914) was the prototype of both the U.S. and British sea-going patrol planes of World War I, and Curtiss flying boats were the only U.S.-built planes used for combat in that war.

A Curtiss flying boat, the giant NC-4, helped win aviation immortality for the Navy on May 16–17, 1919, with the first air crossing of the Atlantic. The NC-4, with its four Liberty engines and 126-foot wingspread, carried a crew of six, headed by Lieutenant-Commander Albert C. Read, from Newfoundland to England, with stops in the Azores and Portugal. It was one of four such craft ordered in 1917 when the Navy decided that, to avoid enemy submarines, it needed flying boats large enough to be delivered overseas by flight rather than by ship.

The 1920s saw Naval Aviation take giant strides in technical progress, operational innovations, and overall gains in size and strength. The radial air-cooled engine brought new efficiency and reliability, helping Navy planes set world records for speed, range, and endurance. The aircraft carrier appeared,

Huge four-engine NC-4 flying boat made historic first air crossing of Atlantic in 1919.

along with specialized carrier-based planes, ship-based seaplanes (launched by catapult), and improved patrol planes (both land- and sea-based).

The techniques of dive-bombing, torpedo attack, scouting, and spotting for gunfire were developed. The lighter-than-air arm took a dramatic turn with the introduction of mammoth dirigibles. Navy pilots applied their skills to photographic survey and even to polar exploration.

In the early 1920s U.S. Navy pilots, flying Curtiss racers, swept the international speed competitions—the Pulitzer and Schneider Trophy races. In November of 1923 Lieutenants Al Williams and Harold Brow took turns setting world speed records.

Single-engine Boeing and Curtiss fighters, powered by the new Pratt & Whitney Wasp, a radial, air-cooled engine, brought dramatic gains in climb and maneuverability. Best known was the Boeing F4B which, in various models, served as the standard Navy and Marine Corps fighter of the late 1920s and

Boeing F4B-1 fighter of 1928 was first of highly successful F4B series which served Navy and Marine Corps aviation for ten years.

Final and most popular model of the F4B series was this F4B-4 fighter of 1931 which had a top speed of 187 mph. The Navy flew 71 F4B-4s, the Marine Corps 21.

18

early 1930s. Technical advances were seen also in Douglas and Martin torpedo planes, Loening and Sikorsky amphibians, and Consolidated flying boats. An outstanding advance in 1927 was the Wasp-powered Vought O2U Corsair, used both for observation and dive-bombing, which continued in service into the mid-1930s.

The Navy's first aircraft carrier, the U.S.S. *Langley*, a converted collier, was commissioned on May 30, 1922, as the CV-1 (C for carrier, V for fixed-wing aircraft). The 11,000-ton, 542-foot *Langley* carried 34 aircraft and served as an experimental ship. In July of 1922 the Navy was authorized to complete two battle cruisers, the *Lexington* and *Saratoga*, as aircraft carriers, and these big vessels, each 888 feet long and displacing 33,000 tons, joined the fleet in the winter of 1927. Each was fitted to carry four squadrons (72 planes), but by 1929 the *Lexington* was putting to sea with 120 fighters and bombers aboard.

Navy's first carrier, the *Langley*, was a converted collier. Planes on deck are Vought VE-7s.

Dirigible *Los Angeles* was flown with great success. Plane making a hook-on landing is a Vought UO-1.

The Navy bought five dirigibles, four of which crashed with 124 lives lost and 116 survivors: the British-built ZR-1 crashed on a test flight in England in 1921; the ZR-2, the American-built *Shenandoah*, launched in 1923, broke up in a thunderstorm over Ohio in 1925; the German-built ZR-3, flown to the United States in 1924 and named the *Los Angeles*, was operated with great success for seven years and was scrapped in 1939; the Goodyear-built ZR-4 (*Akron*) and the ZR-5 (*Macon*), built in 1931 and 1933 respectively, crashed at sea in weather-related accidents.

The dirigible disasters marked the only serious setback in Naval Aviation progress. Still, the decision to use the huge rigid airships made sense at the time, for they had ten times the range and far greater load-carrying capacity than contemporary airplanes, along with speeds three times better than the fastest surface vessel. In addition, the *Akron* and *Macon* each had hangar space for five fighter planes which they could launch and retrieve by means of skyhooks. All these qualities seemed to promise much help to the Navy in its job of patrolling the vast expanses of two oceans.

The Depression slowed Naval Aviation in the early 1930s. Operations were reduced and research and development programs suffered through lack of money. Later, however, with the advent of public works programs under the Roosevelt administration's New Deal, more money became available and Naval Aviation grew again with new planes, new ships, and modernization of Naval Air stations.

Tactics first tried in the 1920s became routine. Three new aircraft carriers (*Ranger, Yorktown*, and *Enterprise*) joined the fleet. Technological advances were seen in new long-range patrol flying boats, retractable landing gear for fighters, supplanting of biplanes with monoplanes, development of new hydraulic arresting gear for stopping planes on carrier decks as well as hydraulic catapults for launching them from the decks, use of new and more accurate bomb sights, and the use of recovery nets (or plane traps) to catch and hold float planes for hoisting aboard ship. Flight training and ground school programs were improved and streamlined with total training periods cut roughly in half.

As a result of these and other advances, the Navy, strongly supported by its air arm, was patrolling the

The carriers *Saratoga*, shown here, and the *Lexington* were built on battle cruiser hulls, and joined the fleet in 1927. Airplanes on flight deck are O2U-1 Corsairs.

Grumman F2F-1 of mid-1930s was first Navy fighter with retractable landing gear.

Atlantic seaboard with essentially the same procedures and equipment soon to be called upon by World War II. Either in development or operation were such mainstay aircraft as the Grumman F4F Wildcat fighter and TBF Avenger torpedo bomber; the Douglas SBD Dauntless dive bomber and TBD Devastator torpedo bomber; the Curtiss SB2C Helldiver dive bomber and SOC Seagull scout seaplane; the Vought OS2U Kingfisher scout seaplane and SB2U Vindicator dive bomber; and a line of big flying boats, including the twin-engine Consolidated PBY Catalina and four-engine PB2Y Coronado, and the twin-engine Martin PBM Mariner. Meanwhile two new high-performance fighters, the Grumman F6F Hellcat and the gull-winged Vought F4U Corsair, both destined for leading roles in World War II, were almost ready for their first flights.

Opposite: Monoplane fighters replaced biplanes with arrival of Grumman F4F Wildcats in late 1930s. Wildcats helped Navy hold the line in early days of World War II before appearance of larger, more powerful fighters.

"Yellow Peril" primary trainer of World War II was familiar to thousands of Naval aviators. This is a Stearman-built N2S-3.

THE "YELLOW PERIL"
NAS CORPUS CHRISTI
1942

Incomparable Consolidated PBY Catalina flying boats served for reconnaissance, rescue, submarine patrol, bombing, and support of ground troops. Shown here is a PBY-5A amphibian.

Consolidated PB2Y Coronados had many roles in World War II, including patrol, transport, search and rescue, and bombing.

Gull-winged Martin PBM Mariners were flown for a variety of missions. They were especially effective against submarines in the Atlantic.

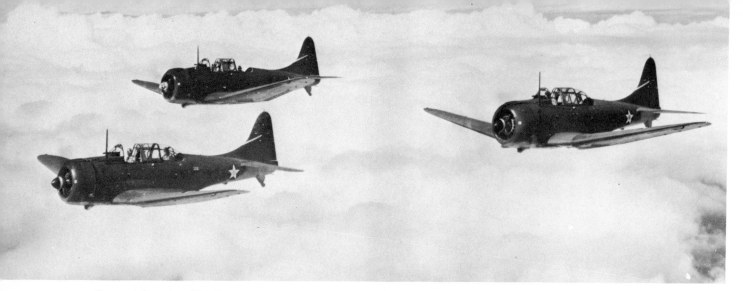

Rugged Douglas SBD Dauntless dive bomber was among Navy combat aircraft ready at the outbreak of World War II.

Naval Aviation proved its worth in World War II. Badly smashed by the surprise Japanese attack on Pearl Harbor, the Navy regrouped and fought back in a two-ocean war. In the Atlantic the job was mainly to protect ships carrying equipment and reinforcements to the Allies, and raw material to U.S. factories. In the Pacific the task was larger and looked almost overwhelming: first, halt the enemy's far-flung advances and, second, drive him homeward across the vast, island-dotted sea. Aviation proved indispensable to the Navy's accomplishment of its missions in both oceans.

Luckily no carriers had been lost at Pearl Harbor, all being at sea when the attack came. Thus it was carrier forces which helped the nation take its first steps on the long road to victory. A carrier force stopped the Japanese at the Battle of the Coral Sea, May 4–8, 1942, the first Naval battle in history in which the opposing ships made no contact. Then, at the Battle of Midway Island, June 3–6, the Navy struck the first blow of retaliation when planes from the carriers *Yorktown, Hornet,* and *Enterprise* sank four Japanese carriers, a heavy cruiser, and destroyed 258 aircraft, a victory which turned the tide of the Pacific war.

Grumman TBF Avenger torpedo bombers, in service at outbreak of World War II, served with distinction throughout the war.

After that, U.S. industrial might and technical advances (seen in thousands of new and improved aircraft), military improvements and growth (shown in fast carrier task forces manned by an air arm of unprecedented size), and an inspired task force leadership (Mitscher, McCain, Halsey, and Spruance, to list but a few of the top names) combined to end the enemy's control of sea and air.

When the war started, Naval Aviation (including the Marine Corps) consisted of seven carriers, 5,233 aircraft, and a total personnel of 27,578 (including 5,900 pilots). By the war's end those totals had grown to 98 carriers, 40,912 aircraft (plus 139 blimps), and a personnel of 430,857 (including 60,095 pilots). Led by such legendary aces as Lieutenant Edward "Butch" O'Hare and Major Gregory "Pappy" Boyington,

Led by two carriers, a task force enters anchorage at Ulithi Atoll for supplies in December, 1944, after strikes against the enemy in the Philippines.

Navy blimp on convoy duty in western Atlantic hovers over merchant ships and scans water for U-boats.

Navy and Marine Corps pilots destroyed more than 15,000 enemy aircraft and sank 174 Japanese warships and 447 Japanese merchant vessels. (The Corsairs and Hellcats proved more than a match for the previously superior Japanese Zero fighters.) The air arm worked not alone but as an integral part of the total Naval force. In the end the war provided practical proof that to control the sea a Navy must first control the air, a truth that the pioneers of Naval Aviation had envisioned over thirty years before.

Postwar demobilization brought quick cuts in Naval air strength. Carriers were retired in "mothball fleets" and planes stored in dry desert areas. Many air stations were closed and within a year the personnel total had fallen to one-fourth of the World War II peak.

Unsung "heroes" of the war in the Pacific, Vought OS2U Kingfishers proved valuable as rescue planes in addition to regular scouting duties.

Martin P5M Marlin, the last of the Navy's long line of flying boats, was operated from 1951 through 1967, giving way to land-based patrol planes during the 1960s.

However, with quantity down, quality climbed as research and development programs were pursued with greater intensity than ever before. Helicopters, jet-powered planes, and guided missiles appeared, all of a growing sophistication and performance which continue to this day. The big flying boats which had served so well in two wars were slowly supplanted by land-based patrol planes of greater speed and range, notably the Lockheed P2V Neptune. (In 1946 a P2V, the *Truculent Turtle*, set a world distance record of 11,236 miles without refueling.) The ballistic missile, Polaris, later to be based aboard submarines as a key weapon of deterrence, was fired for the first time from a ship at sea in August, 1959.

A casualty of the times was the Martin P6M Seamaster, a big, four-jet, sweptwing flying boat, an

Four-engine Martin P6M Seamaster, first successful jet seaplane, had potential to revolutionize Naval Aviation but program was cancelled in 1957 after six had been built.

Lockheed P2V-5F Neptune had two jet engines to assist its two piston engines, carried atomic depth charges and magnetic search gear.

Navy's first production jet, Grumman F9F-2 Panther, was also first Navy jet to enter combat.

imaginative innovation which might have become a competitor to the aircraft carrier, or even to the best land-based bombers. However, by the 1950s, strategic bombing had already been reserved for the U.S. Air Force. Also the advent of the missile-firing submarine made the need for long-range, sea-based aircraft even more questionable. Seamaster development was cancelled in 1959 after a seven-year effort which, though impaired by two accidents, was in the end adjudged a success.

By the late 1940s the last of the Navy's piston-engine fighters were being replaced by jet fighters and fighter-bombers, multimission craft which ended the need for single-purpose torpedo bombers and dive bombers. Several propeller-driven planes (chiefly the venerable Corsair and the newer Douglas AD Skyraider) survived for a time, operating from carriers as low-level bombers and attack planes in the Korean conflict. The Navy's first production jet, the Grumman F9F-2 Panther, became, in Korea, the first

HTL-7 was last of a series of Bell 47 trainer helicopters built for the Navy between 1947 and 1959.

Navy jet to enter combat. Jet fighters, built also by Vought, North American, and McDonnell, evolved into highly successful carrier-based aircraft.

Helicopters, which saw only limited use in World War II, came into their own in Korea for transport and observation. As flying ambulances they saved many lives by speeding the wounded to rear area hospitals. Growing in size, speed, and dependability, helicopters found other uses and won an enduring place in Naval Aviation. At sea they served as rescue-patrol craft, hovering as "plane guards" while planes landed or took off from the carriers. Hovering also enabled them to dip sonar listening devices beneath the sea, a vital part of the Navy's antisubmarine warfare (ASW) efforts. As the years passed, helicopters became minesweepers, cargo carriers from ship-to-shore and ship-to-ship, and (with the Marines) assault transports.

With the advent of the jets and helicopters the operation of seaplanes and blimps ended. Another new element, aviation electronics (avionics) gave the jets and copters further effectiveness. Besides enhancing observation, navigation, communications, and the accuracy of guided missiles, avionics opened up two new systems of vital importance to the Navy—ASW (for fixed-wing planes as well as for helicopters), and airborne early warning (AEW), performed by carrier-based planes packed with electronic gear for long-range detection of aircraft.

To handle the new high-performance aircraft, including supersonic fighters, carriers were modernized with such innovations as the canted flight deck and steam-operated catapults. The first of the new supercarriers, the U.S.S. *Forrestal*, joined the fleet in the 1950s and the world's first nuclear-powered carrier, the U.S.S. *Enterprise*, was commissioned late in 1961, the Golden Year of U.S. Naval Aviation.

Increasingly, Naval Aviation has had a worldwide aspect. Operations High Jump in 1947 and Deep Freeze, starting in 1955–56 and continuing into later years, found the Navy and its air arm in the forefront of Antarctic exploration. On October 31, 1956, seven Navy men landed on the ice at the South Pole in an R4D Skytrain transport plane, the first men to stand there since Captain Robert Scott of the British Royal Navy reached the Pole in January, 1912. In recent years the unstable international situation has kept the Navy on the alert on a global basis—off Africa, Cuba, the Far East, and the Middle East.

The nation's space program of the 1960s found Naval Aviation doing its full share. Throughout the

Lockheed EC-121 Constellations, studded with radar, served for many years, made early warning flights lasting as long as 18 hours. Last one was retired in 1979.

Mercury, Gemini, and Apollo programs, Navy carriers and helicopters were the primary means of recovering the astronauts after they had splashed into the ocean beneath their billowing red and white parachutes. More than half of the American astronauts had Navy backgrounds. On May 5, 1961, Commander Alan B. Shepard became the first American in space. A Marine pilot, Lieutenant-Colonel John Glenn, was the first astronaut to orbit the earth and, in 1969, Apollo 11 astronaut Neil Armstrong, a former Navy pilot, became the first man to walk on the moon.

More recently (April 12–14, 1981) ex-Navy pilots John Young and Robert Crippen flew the space shuttle *Columbia* on its spectacular pioneering voyage into orbit and return to land as a glider.

Associated also with space is the Navy's Polaris missile, a submarine-launched weapon which stands as a prime deterrent to war in this dangerous nuclear age. The Navy was originally authorized to develop the Polaris in December, 1956. The development effort was remarkable by today's standards; from concept to first deployment took only a scant four years.

The success of the program led to improvements in the system and newer, more capable missiles. Polaris itself went to sea in three versions: the A-1, A-2, and finally the A-3 with twice the capability of A-1. Next came the Poseidon missile, which doubled the weight and payload of Polaris, allowing for new, advanced reentry vehicles and multiple warheads. Poseidon fitted onto most of the Polaris submarines. However, the newest missile, the Trident, will fit onto only a few Poseidon submarines and will be carried primarily by the new *Ohio* class of ballistic missile subs. Trident, with its greater range and sophisticated reentry vehicles, is designed to meet the new deterrent needs of the next twenty-five years.

In recent years continued research led to such outstanding current Naval aircraft as the Crusader, Phantom II, and Tomcat fighters; the Skyhawk, Skywarrior, and Corsair II attack planes; the Prowler and Hawkeye for reconnaissance; the Orion long-range patrol plane; and the Sea King, Sea Stallion, and Sea Knight helicopters; each of which, with others, will be covered in the following pages.

We shall look also at new aircraft in development, along with Naval Aviation's future prospects, to see what changes in emphasis and techniques have become possibilities as the twenty-first century draws closer.

Part Two / FIGHTER AIRCRAFT

GRUMMAN F-14 TOMCAT   The F-14 Tomcat is designed to give the U.S. Navy the most advanced air superiority fighter in the world. The Tomcat combines the speed and maneuverability of a dogfighter with a unique electronic weapons control system which enables it to detect and track 24 enemy aircraft and at the same time attack six different aircraft at various altitudes and distances.

The F-14 has three basic missions: 1—fighter sweep escort (clearing contested airspace of enemy fighters and protecting the strike forces); 2—combat air patrol (CAP) and deck-launched intercept (DLI), both in defense of carrier task forces; and 3—attacking ground targets.

The twin-engine, two-seat Tomcat is a "swing-wing" aircraft. With its wings fully extended it can take off in 1,000 feet and land in less than 2,000 feet at speeds under 120 knots (138 mph). With its wings swept back to 68 degrees it flies at speeds above Mach 2 (more than twice the speed of sound). A computer

With its variable-sweep wing folded, Grumman F-14 Tomcat flies over twice the speed of sound.

Heavy load of armament is seen in this underside view of F-14 Tomcat.

swings the wings back automatically, depending on the speed of the craft, thus giving the F-14 the best possible performance for various altitudes and speeds.

The Tomcat was a pioneer aircraft in the use of composite materials which combine high strength with light weight. Its horizontal stabilizer skins were the first composite production parts built for any airplane. Other primary materials in the F-14's structure are titanium (24.4 percent), aluminum alloy (39.4 percent), and steel (17.4 percent).

The F-14's weapons control system is the AWG-9 "track-while-scan" radar built by Hughes Aircraft. The importance of this system is seen in the fact that Phoenix missiles, launched from the Tomcat, have hit targets more than 100 miles away and at altitudes ranging from 50 feet to over 80,000 feet. In 1980 Vice-Admiral W. L. McDonald, Deputy Chief of Naval Operations (Air Warfare), described the F-14/Phoenix combination as "a fighting system without equal in the world today."

In January, 1969, Grumman won a Navy design competition for a new carrier-based fighter known then as the VFX. In December, 1970, the new fighter, the F-14, made its first flight and by the end of 1979 the Navy had 16 F-14 squadrons (with 20 planned) operating from seven carriers and two Naval Air Stations (one on the West Coast and the other on the East Coast). Planned improvements in its engines, missiles, and radar give promise of a long life for the Tomcat.

SPECIFICATIONS AND PERFORMANCE (F-14A)

Manufacturer: Grumman Aerospace Corporation, Calverton, New York

Type: Carrier-based air superiority fighter

Accommodation: Pilot and naval flight engineer

Power plant: Two Pratt & Whitney TF30-P-412A turbofan engines of 20,900 lb. max. static thrust each

Dimensions: Span, wings extended, 64 ft. 1½ in. (19.45 m); fully swept, 39 ft. 2½ in. (11.65 m); length, 61 ft. 11¾ in. (18.89 m); height, 16 ft. (4.88 m); wing area, 565 sq. ft. (52.49 sq. m)

Weights: Empty, 37,500 lb. (17,659 kg); normal takeoff weight, 58,539 lb. (26,553 kg); max. takeoff weight, 74,348 lb. (33,724 kg)

Performance: Max. design speed, Mach 2.4; service ceiling, above 50,000 ft. (15,240 m); min. takeoff distance at normal takeoff weight, 1,200 ft. (366 m); min. field landing distance, 2,000 ft. (600 m); cruise speeds, 460 to 633 mph (740 to 1,018 km/h); approach speed, 138 mph (222 km/h)

Armament: One 20-mm multi-barrel gun; Sparrow and Sidewinder missiles; F-14/Phoenix missile system. Optional: various bombs to total weight of 14,500 lb.

Sweep wing fully extended, Tomcat approaches carrier deck at 138 mph prior to a landing.

39

Twin-jet F-4 Phantom II has served Navy well as a long-range interceptor for over twenty years.

MCDONNELL DOUGLAS F-4 PHANTOM II   One of the finest air weapons ever used by the U.S. Navy is the McDonnell Douglas F-4 Phantom II, a record-breaking aircraft which has been a first line fighter for more than two decades.

The Phantom II (so-named since McDonnell's earlier Navy fighter, the FH-1 Phantom, was no longer in service) was originally designed in 1954 as a twin-engine, long-range, all-weather attack fighter for the Navy under the designation AH-1. Its mission was changed later and when the aircraft entered Naval service in 1960 its designation was F-4B with its chief mission being that of a long-range, high-altitude interceptor.

Over the years the Phantom II proved so successful that it was eventually built in 11 fighter and reconnaissance versions and served with the U.S. Navy, U.S. Marine Corps, U.S. Air Force, and with the air services of eight foreign nations. Production ended in 1979, but the Phantom II remains in operation, the latest Navy models being the F-4J and F-4N.

Year by year continual design improvements and modifications kept the Phantom II in the forefront among the world's fighter aircraft, giving it greater speed, strength, controllability, and overall combat effectiveness. For example—to name but a few advances—the F-4J's two engines each developed 17,850 pounds of thrust compared to 10,900 pounds for the engines of the F-4B. The newer F-4J also had an improved bombing system, a new radar system for more accurate firing of its weapons, and larger wheels to permit a heavier landing weight. As the F-4N, the Phantom II was further improved with the addition of newer avionic equipment, including a computer for plane-to-plane dogfighting. The plane's structure was strengthened for longer life.

The Phantom II first flew on May 27, 1958. Deliveries to Navy and Marine Corps squadrons followed the first carrier-suitability tests in 1960 and by 1966 there were 29 squadrons flying the F-4B, 649 of which had been built.

During its twenty-year-plus career the Phantom II proved its prowess by setting 15 world records for

Hurled by a steam catapult, a Phantom II starts takeoff run along carrier deck.

Phantom II climbs away after a "wave-off" during attempt to land on carrier. Others, foreground, await catapult take-off runs.

speed, altitude, and climb. Included among the marks were 1,606 mph (2,580 km/h) for the 15/25 kilometers course; a flight from Los Angeles to New York, a distance of 2,445 miles, in 2 hours, 48 minutes; and 903 mph (1,453 km/h) for the dangerous 3 kilometers low-level course (maximum altitude 100 meters, or 328 feet). The Phantom II's eight time-to-climb records may probably be best illustrated by the aircraft's amazing zoom from ground level to 9,000 meters (29,528 feet) in only 61.62 seconds.

Among a few of the Phantom II's design and production milestones:

● Production total of 5,195, largest production run of any supersonic fighter in the free world. (The milestone mark of 5,000 was reached in 1978.)

● Total flight time of almost eight-and-a-half million hours for 3,904 aircraft delivered to the U.S. Navy, Marine Corps, and Air Force—equivalent to one aircraft flying continually for 970 years.

● Ability to return safely to base with hydraulic and control systems and one engine completely shot out on either side of aircraft.

● First carrier-based aircraft capable of fully automatic landings.

● A long list of design innovations providing more efficient engine performance, lower stalling speed, improved control at low speeds, and reduced landing speed.

Specifications and Performance (F-4J)

Manufacturer: McDonnell Aircraft Company, a division of McDonnell Douglas Corporation, St. Louis, Missouri

Type: Carrier-based fighter and tactical strike aircraft

Accommodation: Pilot and radar intercept officer

Power plant: Two General Electric J79-GE-10 turbojets of 11,870 lb. static thrust each (17,859 lb. with afterburner)

Dimensions: Span, 38 ft. 4¾ in. (11.7 m); length, 58 ft. 3¾ in. (17.68 m); height, 16 ft. 3 in. (4.95 m); wing area, 530 sq. ft. (49.2 sq. m)

Weights: Empty, 29,641 lb. (13,445 kg); max. takeoff wgt. (carrier or field), 56,000 lb. (25,401 kg); max. landing wgt. (carrier), 38,000 lb. (17,237 kg), (field), 46,000 lb. (20,866 kg)

Performance: Max. speed at sea level without external fuel tanks, 913 mph (1,469 km/h); combat range without external fuel, 1,203 miles (1,936 km); service ceiling, 40,200 ft. (12,060 m); takeoff run (with afterburner), 2,120 ft. (636 m); time to climb (with combat wgt. at max. power), 30,000 ft. (9,000 m) in 51 sec.

Armament: Up to 16,000 lb. (7,258 kg) of missiles, rockets, and bombs on five external attachments

The Navy's "Blue Angels" used F-4s for years in demonstrations of precision aerobatics.

High-performance F-18 Hornet combines fighter and attack capabilities in a single aircraft.

MCDONNELL DOUGLAS F-18 HORNET   The F-18 Hornet is one of the Navy's outstanding aircraft of the future, yet ready to serve today. In taking the steps which eventually led to the Hornet, the Navy, from the outset, sought to combine in a single design a better fighter than the renowned Phantom II and a better attack plane than the A-7 Corsair II. The goal was an aircraft with the high performance and growth potential to serve the U.S. Navy and Marine Corps, as well as other forces of the Western world, into the twenty-first century.

The answer was the F-18A Hornet, a single-seat, twin-jet, dual-mission strike fighter for either carrier- or shore-based operation. As a fighter its chief job is fighter escort and air defense. As an attack aircraft its principal task is stopping enemy ground or sea forces. (In contrast, the F-14 Tomcat, as we have seen, is a twin-seat aircraft whose chief mission is long-range interception.)

The Hornet's origins date back to 1974 when the Navy began to seek proposals for a lightweight, multimission fighter. This led a year later to Navy studies of two designs then being evaluated for the U.S. Air Force: the General Dynamics YF-16 and the Northrop YF-17. The plan was to select one of these designs and adapt it to Navy requirements.

Hornet's twin-jet thrust of 32,-000 pounds exceeds its weight, enables it to accelerate while climbing straight up.

McDonnell Douglas, one of the competing manufacturers, chose the YF-17 as the easiest to convert to carrier operations and, with Northrop, submitted that proposal to the Navy. The Navy approved, and a design development program was carried out during 1975 and 1976. Production contracts followed, with McDonnell Douglas as the prime contractor and Northrop as the major subcontractor. (Assembly and flight testing takes place at the McDonnell Aircraft Company in St. Louis, Missouri.) The Hornet made its first flight on November 18, 1978, and the first production aircraft was delivered in May, 1980.

The F-18A Hornet can fly at nearly twice the speed of sound, maneuver at over 7½ gs (seven and a half times the normal force of gravity), meet hostile aircraft with missiles and cannon fire, and carry 19,000 pounds of armament on nine external attachment points.

The 32,000-pound thrust of the Hornet's two jet engines exceeds the plane's combat weight, so that the F-18A has peak performance no matter where the pilot aims it—including accelerating while climbing straight up. The Hornet's engines have about the same thrust as those in the Phantom II, but are 25 percent shorter, half as heavy, and have 7,700 fewer parts. A Hornet engine can be changed in about twenty minutes, less time than it takes most people to change a flat tire on a car.

A combination of conventional materials (steel and aluminum) and new graphite composite materials give the F-18A the strength to withstand carrier catapult takeoffs and arrested landings. The Hornet's

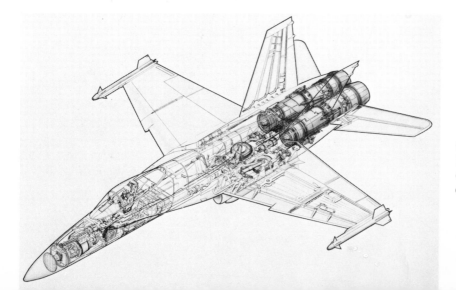

Cutaway drawing of Hornet shows landing gear retracted, aft location of jet engines. F-18 is designed for quick and easy maintenance.

airframe also differs from the YF-17 by having greater wing area, and a larger fuselage to accommodate more fuel and search radar.

The Hornet's twin engines provide an important safety factor: military experience shows that twice as many single-engine planes are lost than twin-engine craft flying the same types of missions. Other Hornet safety features (besides the plane's high speed and agility) include built-in fire extinguishers, self-sealing fuel lines, foam in the wing tanks to suppress explosions, antifire foam filler in the fuselage, and a system for detecting and pinpointing any leaks in the hydraulic lines. The F-18A also has many "backup" systems, the main one being mechanical flight controls for use if anything should happen to the plane's electronic flight controls.

Hornet production rates were relatively low during 1980 and '81, but fully operational F-18A squadrons are expected by late 1982 and early '83. For the long term the Navy and Marine Corps have plans for more than 1,300 Hornets, and Canada for over 130.

The F-18A is designed for growth, with room for new equipment, radar improvements, and more electronics, all vital to the new strike fighter's future—and to greater Naval air strength from now to the year 2000.

SPECIFICATIONS AND PERFORMANCE

Manufacturer: McDonnell Aircraft Company, a division of McDonnell Douglas Corporation, St. Louis, Mo.

Type: Carrier- and land-based Naval strike fighter

Accommodation: Pilot only

Power plant: Two General Electric F404-GE-400 turbojet engines, each of approx. 16,000 lb. (7,258 kg) thrust

Dimensions: Span, 37 ft. 6 in. (11.43 m); span, wings folded, 25 ft. (7.62 m); length, 56 ft. (17.07 m); height, 15 ft. 4 in. (4.59 m); wing area, 400 sq. ft. (37.16 sq. m)

Weights: Takeoff wgt., fighter mission, 33,585 lb. (15,234 kg); max, takeoff wgt., more than 44,000 lb. (19,960 kg)

Performance: Max. level speed, more than Mach 1.8; cruise speed, more than Mach 1; landing approach speed, 150 mph (240 km/h); combat ceiling, 50,000 ft. (15,240 m) approx.; takeoff run, less than 1,000 ft. (305 m); combat radius, over 460 miles (740 km)

Armament: Two Sidewinder heat-seeking missiles; four Sparrow radar-guided air-to-ground missiles; air-to-ground rockets; 20-mm cannon in nose; (19,000 lb. max. load of under-wing and under-fuselage weapons)

Part Three / ATTACK AIRCRAFT

VOUGHT A-7E CORSAIR II   It would be difficult to imagine an aircraft better suited to carry on the proud name of Corsair than the A-7E Corsair II. (The name, first used in 1927, won additional luster with the famous F4U Corsair fighters of World War II.)

This relatively small, single-engine, single-seat aircraft, combat-proven in the Vietnam conflict, combines unprecedented attack accuracy with an armament-carrying ability (15,000 pounds) equal to that of the Allies' big four-engine bombers of World War II and 15 times greater than that of the German Stuka dive bomber. The A-7A is, in the words of one objective expert, "simply a remarkable aircraft." Its many virtues also include long range—over 3,000 miles without refueling—and the ability to "loiter" in an area of attack for more than two hours even while carrying a heavy load of armament.

The Corsair II traces its beginnings back to February, 1964, when the Vought A-7 design was chosen

Vought A-7E Corsair has long been the Navy's main light attack aircraft.

Formation of A-7Es operating from aircraft carrier *Enterprise*.

the winner of a Navy competition for a new plane to replace the Douglas A-4 Skyhawk for the attack and close support missions. The A-7A (first flight September 27, 1965, and first combat December 4, 1967) was followed by three other models for the Navy—the A-7B, A-7C, and the newest, A-7E. The latter first flew on November, 25, 1968, and saw combat from May, 1970, to the end of the war in Southeast Asia. Two other models were also built, the A-7D for the U.S. Air Force and the A-7H for the Hellenic (Greek) Air Force. In all, Vought built about 1,500 A-7 aircraft.

The Corsair II is a subsonic airplane, so-designed after Navy studies had shown that attack and close support missions do not require the supersonic speeds (and extra costs) needed for high-altitude fighter/interceptor missions.

The A-7E's pinpoint accuracy in navigation and low-altitude attacks, even in instrument weather and at night, is made possible by such devices as forward-looking radar and various instrument panel displays which, directed by a central digital computer, give the pilot continuous information on his precise position

Forward-looking infrared radar pods in these A-7Es help provide pinpoint accuracy even in fog or at night.

in relation to the target and the terrain ahead. In brief, the equipment brings the target right onto the pilot's dashboard and the computer tells him when to deliver his bombs, rockets, or missiles. This ultrasophisticated combination is known as the plane's integrated computerized Navigation/Weapons Delivery System (NWDS).

Because of its stubby appearance and ability to bomb and strafe close to friendly ground forces and hit target with extreme accuracy, the Corsair II won the nickname "short, little, ugly fella." The A-7s were also used for bomber escort, search and rescue, minelaying, and as aerial tankers.

Although due to be replaced in the mid-1980s by a new fighter/attack plane (the F-18 Hornet), the A-7E remains as the chief strike weapon of today's Navy carriers, with 26 squadrons in operation. The Corsair II is also used by several reserve units. At any given time the carriers and their air crews form a first line of defense, on the alert in the world's oceans.

Manufacturer: Vought Corporation, a subsidiary of LTV Corporation, Dallas, Texas

Type: Carrier-based light attack bomber

Accommodation: Pilot only

Power plant: One Allison TF41-A-2 (Rolls Royce Spey) non-afterburning turbofan jet engine of 15,000 lb. (6,804 kg) static thrust

Dimensions: Span, 38 ft. 9 in. (11.8 m); length, 46 ft. 1½ in. (14.1 m); height, 16 ft. ¾ in. (4.9 m); wing area, 375 sq. ft. (34.83 sq. m)

Weights: Empty, 19,404 lb. (8,800 kg); max. takeoff, 42,000 lb. (19,050 kg)

Performance: Max. speed at sea level, 691 mph (1,112 km/h); takeoff run at max. takeoff wgt., 5,000 ft. (1,525 m); ferry range with max. internal and external fuel, 3,224 miles (5,188 km)

Armament: One 20-mm multi-barrel gun; various combinations of missiles (Sidewinder, Bullpup, Maverick, Shrike) and bombs up to a total of 15,000 lb. (6,805 kg)

GRUMMAN A-6E INTRUDER

The A-6E Intruder is another excellent example of the military miracles made possible by electronics. Highly sophisticated systems of radar, computers, armament control, and television-type displays enable the A-6E to find, identify, track, and destroy ground targets in any weather, day or night.

This two-seat, twin-jet aircraft, whose chief jobs are close air support and strike missions, has instrument panel displays that show the various heights of the ground out to 10 miles ahead of the plane, enabling the pilot to follow the terrain and avoid obstacles while flying low-level attacks.

The most up-to-date version of the Intruder, the A-6E/TRAM (for Target Recognition Attack Multisensor) contains infrared and laser equipment which provides even greater accuracy. The Intruder can carry more than 30 types of bombs, rockets, and missiles up to a total capacity of 18,000 pounds (8,165 kilograms). The bombardier-navigator (he sits to the pilot's right, but slightly behind and below) operates the weapons delivery system, allowing the pilot to concentrate on the flight and tactical decisions needed for a successful mission.

The A-6E traces its beginnings back to December 31, 1957, when the Grumman design was judged the best of 11 designs submitted in a U.S. Navy competition to develop a carrier-based, low-level attack

51

bomber able to deliver either nuclear or conventional weapons on targets completely hidden by weather or darkness.

The initial Intruder, the A-6A, made its first flight on April 19, 1960, and later saw extensive service in Vietnam. The A-6A was followed by several variants, most of them converted from A-6As already built: the EA-6A (with partial strike capability, but primarily to find, identify, record, and jam enemy electronic communications), the EA-6B Prowler (to be discussed in Part Four/Reconnaissance Aircraft), the A-6B, A-6C, KA-6D (an aerial tanker), A-6E, and finally the specialized version of the A-6E, the A-6E/TRAM. By early 1981 Grumman had built more than 600 A-6 type aircraft and more were planned for the next five years.

Each of the various A-6 models possessed increased effectiveness for attack, or had the additional equipment required for other specialized missions. The most significant advance was the A-6E, chiefly because of a new single, multi-mode navigation and attack radar which replaced the two radar systems in the A-6A and the other earlier models. Eventually all the A-6A variants were converted to the A-6A/TRAM configuration or into KA-6D tankers. The tanker version can transfer 21,000 pounds (9,500 kilograms) of fuel to other aircraft immediately after takeoff, or 15,000 pounds (6,800 kilograms) at a distance of 288 miles (463 kilometers) from its carrier base.

The Intruder carries a heavier and more varied load of armament than any previous U.S. Navy attack aircraft. Like the Corsair II, it is a subsonic aircraft.

Low-altitude support and strike missions are chief jobs of Grumman A-6E Intruder.

Advanced models of Intruders give pilot and bombardier TV-type pictures of targets invisible to eye or radar.

SPECIFICATIONS AND PERFORMANCE (A-6E)

Manufacturer: Grumman Aerospace Corporation, Bethpage, New York

Type: Carrier-based attack bomber

Accommodation: Pilot and bombardier/navigator

Power plant: Two Pratt & Whitney J52-P-8A turbojet engines of 9,300 lb. (4,117 kg) static thrust each

Dimensions: Span, 53 ft. (16.15 m); span (wings folded), 25 ft. 9 in. (7.72 m); length, 54 ft. .9 in. (16.69 m); height, 16 ft. 2 in. (4.93 m)

Weights: Empty, 26,850 lb. (12,179 kg); max. takeoff wgt. (catapult), 58,600 lb. (26,580 kg); max. takeoff wgt. (field), 60,400 lb. (27,397 kg); max. landing wgt. (carrier), 36,000 lb. (16,329 kg); max. landing wgt. (field), 45,000 lb. (20,411 kg)

Performance: Max. speed (sea level), 643 mph (1,035 km/h); cruise speed at best altitude, 476 mph (766 km/h); takeoff run (no armament), 2,350 ft. (716 m); landing run (no armament), 1,900 ft. (579 m); ferry range, 2,737 miles (4,404 km)

Armament: On five attachment points: thirty 500-lb. (226.8 kg) bombs in clusters of six; or three 2,000-lb. (1,633 kg) bombs plus two 300-gallon (1,135 liters) drop tanks; or various rockets, missiles, and mines

At 82,000 pounds, Douglas A-3D Skywarrior is largest and heaviest aircraft to operate from a carrier.

DOUGLAS A-3D SKYWARRIOR

Not long after World War II the Navy envisioned a new mission to add to its offensive air roles—strategic strikes, a mission previously reserved for giant superbombers flying from land bases. The combination of jet engines and nuclear weapons opened the door to this new function for Naval aircraft, and thus was born the Douglas A-3D Skywarrior.

The Navy's concept for the new job called for a bomber to operate from large carriers of the *Midway* class which, in 1947, were in the planning stage. By 1949 the Douglas design to meet this requirement was the Skywarrior, a plane of more than 60,000 pounds gross weight, the largest and heaviest ever proposed for carrier operation. The design included a pressurized cockpit for a three-man crew, a bomb bay to carry 12,000 pounds of bombs (either nuclear or conventional), and, as the only defense, two 20-mm guns in a radar-controlled turret in the tail.

The Skywarrior, with its engine pods slung beneath swept-back wings, had the general look of today's larger executive jets. When it first flew on October 28, 1952, as the XA-3D-1 (one of two prototypes) it was powered by two Westinghouse XJ40 turbojet engines of 7,000 pounds thrust each. The J40 engine program was later abandoned, however, and Pratt & Whitney turbojets of 9,700 pounds thrust each were installed. The XA-3D-1 with the new engines made its first flight on September 16, 1953, and on March 31, 1956, five A-3D-1s flew from the Naval Air Test Center, Patuxent River, Maryland, to a heavy attack squadron at the Naval Air Station, Jacksonville, Florida, the first delivery of Skywarriors to a fleet unit.

The A-3D-1 (later called the A-3A) was used to study the overall concept of carrier-based strategic bombers, along with the problems of operating such large aircraft at sea. Fifty A-3As were built.

The most prominent version of the Skywarrior, the A-3D-2, joined the fleet in 1957 and eventually 164 were built for operation with heavy attack squadrons from carriers of the *Essex* and *Midway* class. The J57 engines in the new Skywarrior had substantially more thrust than the earlier J57 types.

Other Skywarrior versions were produced as photo/reconnaissance aircraft with the bomb bays removed. Included was the RA-3B which equipped two heavy photographic squadrons and which had the entire fuselage pressurized to accommodate two reconnaissance specialists and 12 cameras. Another version, the EA-3B, also had a pressurized fuselage and carried, besides the flight crew, four electronic specialists and devices for radar countermeasures and electronic surveillance missions. Still another model was the TA-3B, a training aircraft carrying six radar/navigation students with an instructor and pilot.

Skywarriors served in Vietnam, primarily as aerial tankers and reconnaissance aircraft.

SPECIFICATIONS AND PERFORMANCE (A-3D-2)

Manufacturer: Douglas Aircraft Company, El Segundo, California

Type: Carrier-based attack bomber

Accommodation: Crew of three

Power plant: Two Pratt & Whitney J57-P-10 turbojets of 12,400 lb. (5,625 kg) static thrust each

Dimensions: Span, 72 ft. 6 in. (21.75 m); length, 74 ft. 4 in. (22.29 m); height, 22 ft. 9½ in. (6.8 m); wing area, 812 sq. ft. (75.43 sq. m)

Weights: Empty, 34,409 lb. (15,608 kg); gross, 82,000 lb. (37,195 kg)

Performance: Max. speed, 610 mph (982 km/h) at 10,000 ft. (3,000 m); service ceiling, 41,000 ft. (12,300 m); tactical radius, 1,050 miles (1,690 km)

Armament: Internal space for up to 12,000 lb. (5,443 kg) of bombs; two 20-mm guns in radar-controlled rear turret

Simplicity was the goal with the Douglas A-4 Skyhawk, which has seen long service as a single-seat, single-engine, single-purpose combat aircraft.

DOUGLAS A-4 SKYHAWK   Sometimes referred to as "Heinemann's Hot Rod" (for its chief designer, Edward Heinemann), the Douglas A-4 Skyhawk is an excellent example of the success possible with a simple, lightweight design built for a specific mission.

Douglas engineers, concerned with the increasing weight and complexity of combat airplanes, decided to "think small" when they went to the drawing board for a jet-powered successor to the big propeller-driven AD-1 Skyraider, an earlier Douglas attack plane which carried a two-man crew. The result was the single-seat Skyhawk, a compact little aircraft which, when originally designed in 1950-52, had a gross weight only half of the 30,000 pounds specified by the Navy for a new attack plane.

The Skyhawk's low wing is of triangular (delta) shape, a sturdy structure, a single piece from tip to tip. Fuel tanks are set in the wing, with additional fuel in the fuselage back of the pilot. Electronics are in the

56

nose. The rear of the fuselage can be detached to allow easy access to the engine for inspection and maintenance.

So effective was the Skyhawk that the Navy eventually bought more than 2,000 in six attack versions. By 1968 Skyhawks were operating from carriers with 30 Navy and Marine Corps squadrons and proved to be vital air weapons during the Vietnam War.

As Skyhawk production moved through the A-4A, B, C, D, E, and F models from 1956 into the late 1960s, continual design changes brought gains in performance and usefulness. More power, for example, came from replacing the Sapphire engine (a British turbojet built under license in the United States by Wright Aeronautical as the J65) with the Pratt & Whitney J52 turbojet. One model, the J52-6A, also provided better fuel mileage, increasing the range of the A-4E Skyhawk by 27 percent.

Other modifications gave the Skyhawk in-flight refueling, a stronger fuselage, limited all-weather capability, radar in the nose, improved avionics, more armament, and better safety with a new "Escapac" ejection seat for the pilot.

Skyhawks were also produced for the Navy as two-seat advanced trainers under the designations TA-4E and TA-4F. The final attack version, the A-4M, went to the Marine Corps, with first deliveries in 1971. Other Skyhawk variants went to five foreign nations and by 1975 total Skyhawk production topped 3,000.

SPECIFICATIONS AND PERFORMANCE (A-4M)

Manufacturer: Douglas Aircraft Company, El Segundo, California

Type: Carrier-based attack bomber

Accommodation: Pilot only

Power plant: One Pratt & Whitney J52-P-408A turbojet of 11,200 lb. (5,080 kg) static thrust

Dimensions: Span, 27 ft. 6 in. (8.25 m); length, 40 ft. 3¾ in. (12.08 m); height, 10 ft. (3 m); wing area, 260 sq. ft. (24.15 sq. m)

Weights: Empty, 10,465 lb. (4,747 kg); gross, 24,500 lb. (11,113 kg)

Performance: Max. speed at sea level, 670 mph (1,078 km/h); initial rate of climb, 8,440 ft./min. (2,532 m); tactical radius with 4,000-lb. bomb load, 340 miles (547 km)

Armament: Two 20-mm guns in the wings; up to 9,155 lb. (4,153 kg) of bombs, missiles, rockets, and fuel tanks on five attachment points under the wings and fuselage

Part Four / RECONNAISSANCE AIRCRAFT

GRUMMAN EA-6B PROWLER   The EA-6B Prowler is the first U.S. Navy aircraft designed and built specifically for tactical electronic warfare. As such, its primary mission is to protect fleet surface vessels and aircraft by jamming enemy radars and radio communications. Its secondary missions include electronic surveillance, antiship missile defense, and the training of radar operators in electronic countermeasures.

The Prowler, which has the same basic design as the A-6 Intruder (described earlier), was lengthened by four and a half feet to make space for a four-seat cockpit—two more than used in the Intruder. The two additional crewmen are required to operate the Prowler's more advanced electronic equipment. Other changes include a pod-shaped antenna fairing atop the vertical fin, more powerful J52-P-408 engines, and a stronger airframe structure.

The EA-6B Prowler tactical jamming system joined the fleet in January, 1971, and was first deployed to Southeast Asia in June, 1972. The Prowler carries no armament, as such, its "weapon" being its

Electronic jamming devices of Grumman EA-6B Prowler have ten times the power of previous systems. The Prowler is vital to defense of the fleet.

electronic jamming devices which have ten times the power of previous systems. Five powered pods with a total of ten jamming transmitters can be carried aboard the EA-6B. Each pod covers one of seven frequency bands, and the Prowler can carry any mix of pods or fuel tanks, depending on the purpose and duration of the mission.

Sensitive surveillance receivers in the tail fin pod can detect enemy radars at long distances. The information is then fed to a central digital computer which processes the signals for display and recording. Detection, identification, direction-finding, and jamming may be performed either automatically or by the crew.

In the latest improved capability configuration (I-CAP), two electronic countermeasures officers (ECMOs) operate the jammers from the Prowler's aft cockpit. Either ECMO can independently detect, assign, adjust, and monitor the jammers. The ECMO in the right front seat is responsible for communications, navigation, and defensive electronic countermeasures.

Grumman and the Navy are continuing to develop improvements in the EA-6B's electronics system to cope with advances in enemy radars. Many Navy and Marine Corps squadrons are now equipped with the new I-CAP versions of the EA-6B and the Prowler is scheduled to remain a vital link in the fleet's first line of defense through the 1980s.

SPECIFICATIONS AND PERFORMANCE (EA-6B)

Manufacturer: Grumman Aerospace Corporation, Bethpage, New York

Type: Carrier- or land-based advanced electronic countermeasures (ECM) aircraft

Accommodation: Pilot and three electronic countermeasures officers (ECMOs)

Power plant: Two Pratt & Whitney J52-P-408 turbojet engines of 11,200 lb. (5,080 kg) thrust each

Dimensions: Span, 53 ft. (16.15 m); span (wings folded), 25 ft. 9 in. (7.72 m); length, 59 ft. 5 in. (18.11 m); height, 16 ft. 3 in. (4.95 m)

Weights: Empty, 32,162 lb. (14,589 kg); max. takeoff wgt. (carrier or field), 65,000 lb. (29,483 kg); max. landing wgt. (carrier or field), 45,500 lb. (20,638 kg)

Performance: Max. level speed, 623 mph (1,002 km/h); max. cruising speed, 605 mph (973 km/h); cruising speed at best altitude, 481 mph (774 km/h); takeoff run, 2,670 ft. (814 m); landing run, 2,150 ft. (655 m); ferry range, 2,022 miles (3,254 km)

Armament: None

GRUMMAN E-2C HAWKEYE   With its distinctive 24-foot-diameter rotating radome and 10,000 pounds of the latest electronic equipment, the E-2C Hawkeye can oversee three million cubic miles of air space. That means, for example, that an E-2C, flying over New York City, can track all the air traffic in the Boston-to-Washington air corridor, the most congested air space in the nation.

The Hawkeye's primary mission is defense. From its operating altitude of about 30,000 feet, this all-weather Airborne Early Warning (AEW) command and control aircraft overcomes the limitations imposed on ground-based radar systems by the earth's curvature. Its advanced radar processing system enables the Hawkeye to automatically detect, identify, and track enemy aircraft, over both land and water, at distances of almost 300 miles, and also to keep a close watch on the movement of enemy ships and land vehicles. The system also detects enemy radar emissions, both surface and airborne, at even greater distances.

The E-2C's long-range radar, through computers, provides information to air defense centers where command decisions are made. The E-2C also controls friendly aircraft, enabling them to make pinpoint interceptions of enemy aircraft. The system can handle more than 600 tracks over land and water, providing such information as course, speed, altitude, and identification of all the targets picked up by its radar.

The rugged Hawkeye is the latest of five generations of Airborne Early Warning aircraft built by Grumman since the mid-1940s. At that time a TBF Avenger torpedo bomber was modified with the first-generation airborne search radar. This was followed in the mid-1950s by the E-1B. In 1964 the Navy received the first aircraft designed specifically for AEW, the E-2A Hawkeye, 59 of which were delivered through 1967. They flew in Vietnam combat from aircraft carriers. The E-2As were modified to E-2Bs with a new high-speed digital computer.

The third-generation Hawkeye, the E-2C, made its first flight in January, 1971, and the first

Revolving radar radome, 24 feet in diameter, is distinguishing mark of Grumman E-2C Hawkeye Airborne Early Warning aircraft. Flying at high altitudes, Hawkeye can monitor 30 million cubic miles of air space.

operational aircraft were delivered to the Navy in 1973. By the end of 1978, 45 Navy E-2C Hawkeyes were delivered. In all, more than 100 Hawkeyes have been built, with production scheduled for several more years.

The Hawkeye has the highest operational ready rate of any carrier aircraft in the U.S. Navy, meeting well over 90 percent of its scheduled missions. Approximately 80 percent of the Hawkeyes, returning from missions, are ready to fly again immediately after refueling.

Powered by twin turboprop engines, the Hawkeye combines good fuel economy with short-takeoff runs, and can cruise on station for four hours, 200 miles from its base. This mission time can be increased to nine hours with fuel tanks added in the outer sections of the wings. In addition, an in-flight refueling probe can be installed, giving far greater cruise time.

With its five-man crew, the Hawkeye is designed to eliminate surprise attacks, not only by bombers and fighters, but from low-altitude airplanes, helicopters, and missiles, as well as by ships and ground vehicles.

SPECIFICATIONS AND PERFORMANCE (E-2C)

Manufacturer: Grumman Aerospace Corporation, Bethpage, New York

Type: Carrier- or land-based Airborne Early Warning aircraft

Accommodation: Pilot, copilot, radar operator, air control operator, and combat information center operator

Power plant: Two Allison T56-A-425 turboprop engines of 4,910 hp (3,661 kw) each; two 4-bladed Hamilton Standard propellers, foam-filled and with steel spar and fiber glass shells for minimum radar interference

Dimensions: Span, 80 ft. 7 in. (24.56 m); length, 57 ft. 7 in. (17.55 m); height, 18 ft. 4 in. (5.59 m); propeller diameter, 13 ft. 6 in. (4.11 m); wing area, 700 sq. ft. (65.03 sq. m)

Weights: Empty, 37,678 lb. (17,090 kg); max. takeoff wgt., 51,569 lb. (23,391 kg)

Performance: Max. level speed, 361 mph (581 km/h); cruise speed, 302 mph (486 km/h); landing speed, 107 mph (172 km/h); service ceiling, 30,800 ft. (9,390 m); takeoff run, 1,890 ft. (576 m); ferry range, 1,605 miles (2,583 km)

Armament: None

LOCKHEED EC-130Q HERCULES   The story of the EC-130Q Hercules revolves largely around the highly specialized activities of the Navy's two Fleet Air Reconnaissance Squadrons—VQ-4 based at the Naval Air Station, Patuxent River, Maryland, and VQ-3 operating out of Guam in the Pacific.

Any similarity between these units and other Navy reconnaissance squadrons is in name only. First, their aircraft, the four-engine, land-based Hercules (a type usually flown as aerial tankers and troop and cargo transports), is far larger than carrier-based reconnaissance aircraft. More significant, though, is their mission: for all practical purposes they are mobile communications squadrons operating on an around-the-clock basis.

The primary mission of VQ-4 and VQ-3 is to provide a mobile backup for the Navy's shore-based communications stations in the event of a national emergency. This assures that the Navy's top command, under the direction of the Joint Chiefs of Staff, will always be able to communicate with the missile-

Lockheed EC-130Q Hercules aids communication with Navy's distant missile-bearing submarines—a special mission in event of a national emergency.

bearing submarines which cruise constantly on worldwide alert as the Navy's deployed *strategic* forces.

VQ-4 and VQ-3 are known as TACAMO squadrons, the word being an acronym derived from the Marine Corps challenge to "Take Charge and Move Out." Their C-130 aircraft, modified as EC-130Qs, make use of an improved communications system developed by the Collins Radio Group of Rockwell International Corporation. The first of ten improved EC-130Qs began to reach VQ-4 during 1973.

A brief look at the activities of the VQ-4 squadron reveals the scope and importance of the TACAMO responsibilities. Normal flight operations for the squadron involve independent crew deployments throughout the North Atlantic region. The flights occur on a daily basis and originate from a ring of bases to make sure that there will always be a TACAMO aircraft airborne. This demanding requirement calls for the utmost in aircraft scheduling and reliability. As evidence of its success in performing its JCS-directed mission, VQ-4 customarily logs almost 12,000 flight hours a year with a reliability of 100 percent.

VQ-4 also uses its EC-130Qs to train pilots and air crewmen for both Navy TACAMO squadrons. VQ-4 won the special mission Naval Air Force Battle Efficiency Award in 1974–75 and again in 1977–78. It also won the Chief of Naval Operations Safety Award, Atlantic Fleet, in 1978, and in 1979 was recognized for accumulating 77,000 accident-free flight hours during the preceding seven years—all testimony to the rugged reliability of the Hercules aircraft and the skill of the crews who operate them.

SPECIFICATIONS AND PERFORMANCE

Manufacturer: Lockheed-Georgia Company, Marietta, Georgia

Type: Land-based reconnaissance aircraft as mobile backup for shore-based communications stations in event of national emergency

Accommodation: Pilot, copilot, third pilot, two flight engineers, navigator, and a seven-man communications crew

Power plant: Four Allison T56-A-423 turboprop engines of 4,910 shaft hp each (3,661 kw)

Dimensions: Span, 132 ft. 7 in. (39.8 m); length, 97 ft. 8 in. (29.28 m); height, 38 ft. 3 in. (11.4 m); wing area, 1,745 sq. ft. (162 sq. m)

Weights: Empty, 98,500 lb. (44,680 kg); max. takeoff wgt., 165,000 lb. (74,844 kg)

Performance: Max. cruise speed, 357 mph (574 km/h); long-range cruise speed, 343 mph at 25,000 ft. (552 km/h); range, over 3,000 miles (4,827 km)

Armament: None

SIKORSKY RH-53D SEA STALLION   Another aircraft equipped for a special mission is the RH-53D Sea Stallion, a powerful twin-turbine helicopter and the first Navy rotorcraft designed specifically to serve as a minesweeper.

The RH-53D is a descendant of the CH-53A, an assault transport helicopter first ordered in 1962 for the U.S. Marine Corps. The CH-53A made its flight debut on October 24, 1964, and entered service with the Marines in mid-1966. The CH-53A and an improved model, the CH-53D, saw extensive service in Vietnam as troop and cargo carriers. Production of Sea Stallions for the Marines ended in 1972 with a combined total of 265 A and D models delivered.

In October, 1970, the Navy announced plans to establish mine countermeasures (MCM) squadrons. The first unit, Mine Countermeasures Squadron 12 (HM-12) operated 15 CH-53As on loan from the Marine Corps and equipped with kits for towing the minesweeping gear.

Later the Navy received Congressional approval to develop a new and more powerful version of the CH-53 for service with airborne mine countermeasures squadrons and, in February, 1972, Sikorsky Aircraft received an order for 30 helicopters under the designation RH-53D. The first flight of the new copter came on October 27, 1972, and the first deliveries were made to HM-12 in September, 1973.

Introduction of the big RH-53Ds represented a major step forward in the Navy's MCM activities, for the task of finding and sweeping mines can be carried out with far greater speed and safety by helicopter. When the conventional surface minesweeper enters a mine field it risks destruction by the very mines it is trying to cut adrift. The helicopter, well clear of the water, faces no such danger.

This was graphically shown in two of the most notable minesweeping jobs performed by MCM Squadron HM-12—in Haiphong Harbor in 1973 after the Vietnam War, and in the Suez Canal following the "Yom Kippur" War of 1973. The Suez operation was especially convincing. The 100-mile waterway had been closed since the six-day war of 1967, littered from end to end with the debris of two wars—sunken ships, aircraft wrecks, land vehicles, and bombs. The canal was heavily mined and was blocked in several places by causeways built during the most recent conflict.

Despite these obstacles and the necessity of making long flights from distant bases each day before starting their sweeps, the HM-12 crews, flying 12 new RH-53Ds, cleared the entire canal and six miles of

Sikorsky RH-53D Sea Stallion picks up minesweeping gear during 38-day operation which cleared Suez Canal in 1974.

approach waters in 38 days. Their achievement showed that helicopters can sweep mines with fewer men than surface minesweepers, as well as faster and with greater safety.

The RH-53D is designed to tow present and future equipment for sweeping various types of mines—mechanical, acoustic, and magnetic. The equipment for mechanical and acoustic mines can be carried within the Sea Stallion's cavernous fuselage and deployed from the rear cargo door. When sweeping is completed the gear can be retrieved in flight. The magnetic mine equipment, too large to be carried within the helicopter, is first streamed behind a surface vessel and then engaged by the copter's tow hook. The magnetic sweep equipment can also be carried on the helicopter's external cargo hook, a method used to lift the gear from ship to sea or from shore to sea.

Like its predecessors, the RH-53D can fold its main and tail rotors for stowage aboard aircraft carriers. Beyond that, the minesweeping Sea Stallions differ substantially from the earlier assault transport models. Among the modifications: increased engine power, higher weights, stronger landing gear and brakes, more space for advanced navigation systems, a 500-gallon droppable fuel tank on each sponson, an in-flight refueling probe in the nose, equipment for ship-to-helicopter refueling while in hover, stowage racks and cradles for the MCM devices, a 20,000-pound capacity tow boom, hydraulic winches for streaming and recovering the sweep gear, and additions to the automatic flight control system to meet the special needs of minesweeping.

SPECIFICATIONS AND PERFORMANCE

Manufacturer: Sikorsky Aircraft, a division of United Technologies, Stratford, Connecticut

Type: Carrier-based mine countermeasures helicopter

Accommodation: Pilot, copilot, helicopter crew chief, and MCM crew

Power plant: Two General Electric T64-GE 415 turboshaft engines of 4,380 shaft hp (3,266 kw) each

Dimensions: Rotor diameter, 72 ft. 2¾ in. (21.67 m); length overall, 88 ft. 2⅓ in. (26.5 m); length, rotors folded, 55 ft. 6 in. (16.65 m); height, 17 ft. 1½ in. (5.2 m)

Weights: Normal takeoff wgt., 42,000 lb. (19,050 kg); max. takeoff wgt., 50,000 lb. (22,680 kg)

Performance: Max. speed, sea level, 196 mph (315.4 km/h); cruise speed, 172 mph (278 km/h); best rate of climb, 2,510 ft./min. (753 m); service ceiling, 17,000 ft. (5,182 m); range, 278 miles (448 km)

Armament: Two .50-cal. guns to detonate surfaced mines

VOUGHT RF-8G CRUSADER   The RF-8G is the photo-reconnaissance version of the Vought F-8 Crusader, the last Navy fighter developed by the Chance Vought Aircraft Company before it became part of the Ling-Temco-Vought (LTV) Corporation in 1961.

The RF-8G's heritage from its fighter forebears includes design qualities and supersonic speeds which made the Crusader the backbone of Naval and Marine Corps fighter strength for two decades—from the mid-1950s to the mid-1970s.

Among the Crusader's achievements: the first supersonic crossing of the United States (3 hours, 23 minutes, from Los Angeles to New York, July 16, 1957, in an RF-8A by Major John Glenn, later an astronaut and U.S. Senator); the first national and world speed record over 1,000 miles an hour by a production aircraft (by Commander R. W. "Duke" Windsor in 1956 in an F-8A) which brought the Navy its first Thompson Trophy for the outstanding aviation achievement of the year; winner of the coveted Collier Trophy (to Vought and the Navy) as the first carrier-based fighter to exceed speeds of 1,000 mph); the first coast-to-coast, carrier-to-carrier flight (two F-8s from the U.S.S. *Bon Homme Richard* off the coast of California to the U.S.S. *Saratoga* off the Florida coast).

During the Cuban crisis of 1962 the first of the photo-reconnaissance Crusaders, the RF-8A, played a leading role in detecting Soviet missile sites in Cuba. Navy and Marine Corps pilots dashed high across the island, their cameras grinding, and landed at the Naval Air Station, Jacksonville, Florida, where the films were processed and quickly flown to Washington. There the pictures gave President Kennedy the evidence needed to force withdrawal of the missile threat. For their work the two squadrons involved received Presidential Citations, while the six Navy and four Marine pilots who flew the missions won Distinguished Flying Crosses.

Crusaders flew combat missions in Southeast Asia almost from the outbreak of the hostilities in 1964, operating from shore bases and carriers as fighters, attack, and photo-reconnaissance aircraft.

The Crusader made its first flight March 25, 1955, at Edwards Air Force Base, California, and joined the fleet the following year. One of its design features was a two-position, variable-incidence wing which gave the pilot good visibility by permitting the fuselage to remain level while the wing, rotating on its rear spar, assumed the higher angle of attack necessary for shorter takeoffs and slower landings.

Vought RF-8G Crusader, shown over carrier *Oriskany*, has four camera positions, carries no guns or armament.

For close stowage on flight and hangar decks the outer one-third of each Crusader wing folds upward. As evidence of the Crusader's excellent control and rugged construction there are seven known instances of F-8s taking off with their outer wing sections still folded. (The Crusader's wings are set far back on the fuselage and are not readily visible to the pilot, especially at night.) All seven of the forgetful fliers made safe, although very high-speed, landings, thanks largely to the fact that the ailerons are on the inboard (unfolded) section of the wings. All but one of the "wingless" flights occurred at night and the takeoffs and landings were all made at Navy airfields, the landings being helped by arresting cables on the runways. Six of the seven pilots flew for as long as 45 minutes in their folded-wing planes. The seventh, warned by the control tower just as he became airborne, cut his engine, dropped his tail hook, and successfully engaged the field's arresting cables.

SPECIFICATIONS AND PERFORMANCE

Manufacturer: Vought Corporation, a subsidiary of LTV Corporation, Dallas, Texas
Type: Carrier-based, turbojet reconnaissance aircraft
Accommodation: Pilot only
Power plant: One Pratt & Whitney J57-P-20A turbojet engine of 10,700 lb. (4,854 kg) thrust
Dimensions: Span, 35 ft. 2 in. (10.5 m); length, 54 ft. 6 in. (16.3 m); height, 15 ft. 9 in. (4.7 m); wing area, 350 sq. ft. (32.5 sq. m)

Weights: Mission weight (approx.), 28,000 lb. (12,700 kg); max. gross wgt., 34,000 lb. (15,422 kg)
Performance: Max. speed (at 40,000 ft.), 1,120 mph (1,802 km/h); cruise speed (at 40,000 ft.), 560 mph (901 km/h); rate of climb, 6 min. 30 sec. to 57,000 ft. (17,100 m); service ceiling, 59,000 ft. (17,700 m); range, 1,100 miles (1,770 km)
Armament: None. (Aircraft has four camera stations, each carrying one camera.)

NORTH AMERICAN RA-5C VIGILANTE

The Vigilante, although retired from service in early 1980, merits more than a passing mention in view of its unusual background and record-breaking achievements.

The A-5A Vigilante, a heavily armed attack plane designed to carry nuclear bombs, had its origins in the mid-1950s. The RA-5C Vigilante, an unarmed reconnaissance aircraft, was a descendant of the A-5A.

A major shift in defense policy, the removal of strategic bombing from the Navy's area of responsibility, led to the birth of the RA-5C. As a result of that change, plans to produce an improved Vigilante attack bomber were abandoned after the new design, the A-5B, had reached an advanced stage.

The proposed A-5B had a deeper fuselage to carry more fuel, larger flaps and improved "boundary layer control" (a system for blowing air over the whole wing to provide better lift and control at landing

Retired in 1980, the RA-5C Vigilante, an unarmed reconnaissance plane, was descendant of long-range, high-performance A-5A, originally designed to carry nuclear bombs.

speeds), and two additional underwing pylons (for a total of four) to carry four 400-gallon droppable fuel tanks.

All these improvements were built into the RA-5C. In addition, a large array of electronic and visual reconnaissance equipment occupied the fuselage bomb bay of the original A-5 attack version. Among the reconnaissance devices were side-looking radar, cameras aimed at various angles, and a wide variety of electronic countermeasures (ECM) equipment.

The RA-5C first flew on June 30, 1962. When production topped 90 aircraft in 1964 the Navy added further to the Vigilante reconnaissance total by converting many of the original A-5As to RA-5Cs. The first squadron to receive RA-5Cs operated them from the carrier *Ranger* in 1964.

Achievements of the A-5A provide proof of the later usefulness of the RA-5C: On December 30, 1960, at Edwards Air Force Base, California, an A-5A set a world altitude record of 91,450 feet (over 17 miles) for land-based jet aircraft carrying a payload of 1,000 kilograms (2,204.62 pounds). The record topped by more than four miles the previous mark of 67,096 feet by a Russian twin-jet RV monoplane.

In 1960 at Columbus, Ohio, an A-5A carried Rear Admiral William A. Schoech, deputy chief of the Navy's Bureau of Weapons, to a speed twice the speed of sound, making him the first admiral to fly at Mach 2 speed. Also in 1960 the late Jacqueline Cochran, riding in an A-5A's navigation seat, became the first woman to fly at Mach 2 speeds.

Based either on land or aboard carriers, the original attack Vigilante could carry a variety of nuclear or nonnuclear bombs to distant sea or land targets in any weather at twice the speed of sound, and operating at either very low or high altitudes. The A-5A, with its high, thin sweptwing and long list of design advances, had fully met the Navy's 1955 requirement for "a high-performance attack aircraft with all-weather capability," qualities that later made its offspring, the RA-5C, an outstanding reconnaissance aircraft.

SPECIFICATIONS AND PERFORMANCE (RA-5C)

Manufacturer: North American Aviation (later, Columbus Aircraft Division of Rockwell International), Columbus, Ohio

Type: Carrier-based electronic and visual reconnaissance aircraft

Accommodation: Pilot and observer/radar operator

Power plant: Two General Electric J79-GE-8 turbojets of 10,900 lb. static thrust (4,944 kg) each, without afterburner; and 17,000 lb. (7,711 kg) with afterburner

Dimensions: Span, 53 ft. (15.9 m); length, 76 ft. 6 in. (22.9 m); height, 19 ft. 4 in. (5.8 m); wing area, 754 sq. ft. (70 sq. m)

Weights: Empty, 40,900 lb. (18,552 kg); takeoff gross wgt., 66,800 lb. (30,300 kg)

Performance: Max. speed, Mach 2.1 or 1,385 mph (2,228 km/h) at 40,000 ft. (1,200 m); cruise speed, 1,254 mph (2,018 km/h); combat ceiling, 48,400 ft. (14,520 m); combat radius, up to 1,500 miles (2,414 km)

Armament: None

Part Five / SEARCH AIRCRAFT

LOCKHEED S-3A VIKING The S-3A Viking is the sixth model in a long line of Lockheed aircraft which for more than forty years have carried out the antisubmarine (ASW) mission for the U.S. Navy and other nations.

The Viking's Lockheed predecessors were: the Hudson bomber (1939) which was adapted for many uses, including ASW; the PV-1 Vega Ventura (1941), 1,600 of which were built for the Navy; the PV-2 Harpoon (1944) which saw World War II service in the Pacific; the P2V-1 Neptune (1945) in which were pioneered the integrated ASW systems on which all subsequent U.S. systems were based; and the long-range P-3 Orion (1959), the military version of the four-engine Electra transport.

The S-3A Viking is a compact, stubby-looking monoplane with a towering (and seemingly outsized) tail fin and rudder. It is powered by two turbofan engines attached to pylons beneath its high wing.

Vikings from antisubmarine squadron fly a tight formation. Their job: protect the Navy's carrier fleet.

The Viking's massive array of avionics gear is distributed throughout the aircraft. Sixty sonobuoys (which are dropped into the sea in the search for subs) nestle in launching tubes in the lower section of the fuselage; a forward-looking infrared (FLIR) scanner is installed in a retractable turret atop the fuselage; the nose houses the plane's search and navigation radar; a magnetic anomaly detector (MAD), which warns of the presence of undersea metallic objects, is attached to a retractable boom or "stinger" in the tail; and an electronic support measures system (ESM) has its antennas within small fairings on the wingtips. To provide for future growth and new missions, the fuselage has space for a 50 percent expansion of electronics equipment.

The S-3A dates back to 1969 when Lockheed was awarded a Navy contract to develop a new ASW aircraft to replace the aging Grumman S-2 Tracker, winning out in a competition with four other aircraft companies. The prototype S-3A made its first flight on January 21, 1972, and production orders soon followed. The first Vikings were delivered in February, 1974, to a training squadron at the Naval Air Station, San Diego, California, and the new submarine hunters were first deployed aboard the carrier *John F. Kennedy* in July, 1975. Since then 13 S-3A squadrons have gone aboard carriers in the Atlantic and Pacific. The last of a production total of 187 aircraft was delivered in 1978.

Two types of aircraft, the airplane and the helicopter, with their vastly different capabilities, now complement each other for the ASW mission. Airplanes, having superior speed and range, handle the long-distance searches, while helicopters, able to hover but limited in range by their slower speed, fly the short-distance missions. Speed and range have become increasingly important to the ASW mission in recent years because of the threat of submarines which can launch their nuclear missiles at shore targets from great distances at sea. For this reason the Viking, with its cruise speed of over 400 miles an hour and combat range of more than 2,000 miles, represents competition for the helicopter as a defense against undersea craft, a competition which is likely to increase in the future.

Opposite: Lockheed S-3A Viking nears carrier on approach to a landing. In foreground, another S-3A, with wings and tail folded, rests on elevator to hangar deck.

Manufacturer: Lockheed-California Company (in association with Vought Systems Division of LTV), Burbank, California

Type: Twin-engine, carrier-based, antisubmarine aircraft

Accommodation: Pilot, copilot, tactical coordinator, and sensor operator

Power plant: Two General Electric TF34-GE-2 turbofan engines of 9,275 lb. (4,207 kg) thrust each

Dimensions: Span, 68 ft. 8 in. (20.9 m); span, wings folded, 29 ft. 6 in. (8.9 m); height, 22 ft. 9 in. (6.9 m); height, tail folded, 15 ft. 3 in. (4.65 m); length, 53 ft. 4 in. (16.26 m); length, tail folded, 49 ft. 5 in. (15 m); wing area, 598 sq. ft. (55.5 sq. m)

Weights: Empty, 26,650 lb. (12,088 kg); max. gross wgt., 52,539 lb. (23,831 kg); normal takeoff wgt., 42,500 lb. (19,277 kg); max. landing wgt. (carrier), 37,695 lb. (17,098 kg); max. landing wgt. (field), 45,914 lb. (20,826 kg)

Performance: Max. speed, 518 mph (834 km/h); max. cruise speed, 426 mph (686 km/h); max. combat range, 2,900 miles (4,666 km); loiter endurance, sea level, 7 hours 30 min.; service ceiling, 40,000 ft. (12,000 m); takeoff run, 2,200 ft. (671 m); landing run, 1,600 ft. (488 m); max. rate of climb, 4,200 ft./min. (1,280 m); ferry range, 3,554 miles (3,000 km)

Armament: Internal space for torpedoes, bombs, mines, or depth charges; one attachment under each wing for rockets, missiles, bombs, or auxiliary fuel tanks

SIKORSKY SH-3 SEA KING In the mid-1950s the Navy's use of helicopters as antisubmarine aircraft centered around the single-engine Sikorsky HSS-1 (S-58) which was flown in hunter/killer pairs—one copter carrying the sonar listening devices for detecting submerged subs, and the other armed with depth charges. It was a reasonably good beginning in the operational use of rotary wing aircraft for ASW, but still left much room for improvement.

The improvement was not long in coming: in December, 1957, the Navy contracted with Sikorsky to develop a new helicopter in which the dual role of hunter/killer would be combined. The result, the twin-turbine SH-3A Sea King (50 percent larger and with more than twice the endurance of the HSS-1), the first of a series of SH-3 models that have handled the Navy's helicopter ASW job for more than two decades.

The greater size and power of the SH-3A enabled it to carry instruments for all-weather flight as well as the sonar search gear and almost 850 pounds of weapons. The new craft's watertight hull and two stabilizing floats (into which the copter's landing wheels retracted) made the SH-3A a true amphibian.

Latest Sikorsky Sea King is this SH-3H which carries additional electronic equipment for improved antisubmarine warfare and antiship missile detection.

Unfortunately, however, the engines, mounted atop the fuselage, gave the copter a high center of gravity, making it unstable on the water with its rotor blades not turning. The problem was solved by installing rubber "pop-out" floats which could be deflated in the event of emergency landings on the water.

The SH-3A (known initially as the HSS-2) made its first flight on March 11, 1959, and deliveries to the fleet began in September, 1961. Other models followed as the Sea King, fitted with engines of greater power, gained in performance and, with the addition of various special equipment, evolved into a multipurpose helicopter.

The new Sea King models included:

● The SH-3D (1966), which became the Navy's first-line ASW helicopter, also served with the navies of Spain, Brazil, and Argentina, and was later built under license in England by Westland Helicopter, Ltd.

● The RH-3A (1965), converted from the A model as a minesweeper, with the ASW gear removed and replaced by towing equipment.

77

- The VH-3A and later VH-3D, used as VIP transports and available for emergency evacuation of key government officials, including the President.
- The HH-3A, used for search-and-rescue duties in combat areas, including Vietnam, and later fitted with a system for refueling from surface vessels while hovering, an operation called "high drink." The HH-3A also carried long-range fuel tanks.
- The SH-3G, converted from SH-3A models in 1970 and onwards and used as utility and search-and-rescue aircraft.
- The SH-3H (conversions of A and G models), a multipurpose helicopter which, with the addition of a half dozen new electronic sensors, serves as an antiship missile detector, as well as for antisubmarine duty.

During the U.S. Gemini and Apollo space programs of the 1960s, Sea Kings, flying from carriers in the Atlantic and Pacific, were the primary vehicles for recovering the astronauts from the sea following completion of their earth-orbiting and moon flights.

Technological advances of recent years have brought improved ASW capabilities to both helicopters and fixed-wing airplanes. Yet submarine technology has advanced also, along with the numbers of undersea craft. As one carrier captain expressed it over fifteen years ago, the missile-carrying, nuclear-powered sub is a "real tough nut to crack."

SPECIFICATIONS AND PERFORMANCE (SH-3D)

Manufacturer: Sikorsky Aircraft, a division of United Technologies, Stratford, Connecticut

Type: All-weather antisubmarine helicopter

Accommodation: Pilot, copilot, and two sonar operators

Power plant: Two General Electric T58-GE-10 turboshaft engines of 1,400 shaft hp (1,004 kw) each

Dimensions: Main rotor diameter, 62 ft. (18.9 m); length, 72 ft. 8 in. (22.15 m); length, tail pylon folded, 47 ft. 3 in. (14.4 m); width, rotors folded, 16 ft. 4 in. (4.98 m); height, 16 ft. 10 in. (5.13 m)

Weights: Empty, 12,087 lb. (5,483 kg); ASW mission gross wgt., 18,897 lb. (8,572 kg); max. takeoff wgt., 20,500 lb. (9,300 kg)

Performance: Max. level speed, 166 mph (267 km/h); cruise speed, 136 mph (219 km/h); initial climb, 2,200 ft./min. (670 m); service ceiling, 14,700 ft. (4,480 m); hover ceiling, 8,200 ft. (2,500 m); range, 625 miles (1,005 km); endurance, 4.5 hours (approx.)

Armament: 840 lb. (381 kg) of homing torpedoes and depth bombs

Sea King helicopter recovers
Apollo 8 astronauts, December
28, 1968, following spacecraft's
lunar orbit flight.

Final Kaman Seasprite model, the SH-2F, is a key element in Navy's LAMPS I fleet defense system.

KAMAN SH-2 SEASPRITE   When the Navy held a design competition in 1956 for a new high-performance, all-weather helicopter, it was looking primarily for a search-and-rescue machine, yet one that would also be suited for a variety of other missions. These included reconnaissance, plane guard duties aboard carriers, courier service, gunfire observation, transfer of personnel from ship-to-ship and ship-to-shore, casualty evacuation, and air controller operations.

Kaman Aircraft Corporation won the competition with its compact little H-2 Seasprite which, in various and ever-improving versions, has served the Navy for two decades as a multipurpose aircraft of excellent speed and reliability.

The prototype Seasprite, the single-engine HU2K-1 (later redesignated UH-2A) made its first flight on July 2, 1959. Production deliveries began in late 1962 and early '63 to utility squadrons at the Naval Air Station, Lakehurst, New Jersey, and the Naval Auxiliary Air Station, Ream Field, near San Diego, California. From those bases the UH-2As went aboard carriers in both the Atlantic and Pacific fleets, serving chiefly as plane guards (airborne and ready for instant rescue work during takeoffs and landings of the carriers' fighters and bombers).

Deliveries of UH-2A and B models totaled 190 through 1965. Between 1967 and 1972 all these aircraft were modified as twin-engine helicopters under the designation UH-2C. When the Navy used Seasprites as rescue vehicles in Vietnam the copter was further modified as the HH-2C with increased engine power, a new four-bladed tail rotor, dual-tired main wheels, and the protection of guns and armor plate. The HH-2D which followed had all the improvements except the guns and armor.

In 1970 the Navy, in its constant struggle to improve its antisubmarine effectiveness, decided to

Kaman SH-2F Seasprite, shown leaving helipad on destroyer *Spruance*, has many design, structural, electronic, and power improvements over earlier models.

convert its Seasprites again and base them aboard destroyers for searching out and attacking submarines. This effort was part of the Navy's new Light Airborne Multi-Purpose System (LAMPS) program whose goal was to provide an "over-the-horizon" search-and-attack capability for its ASW destroyer fleet.

The new model, the SH-2D, had a powerful search radar in a radome "tub" under its nose, and additional equipment suitable for either antisubmarine warfare or for defense against antiship missiles. The Seasprite's small size made it ideal for operation from helipads installed at the sterns of the destroyers.

A final Seasprite model, the SH-2F, appeared in 1972, its new features including an improved rotor which virtually eliminated rotor vibration, a simplified rotor control system which reduced by two-thirds the number of control parts, a stronger landing gear, a shortened wheel base (by moving the tail wheel forward) for greater deck edge clearance on the small landing pads, improved electronics, and a higher gross weight.

Modification of the early Seasprite models to the SH-2F configuration was carried to completion throughout the 1970s and the F model continues to serve the Navy's antisubmarine efforts. Except for a few HH-2D rescue aircraft still in operation, the Seasprite's task has now become active defense rather than utility.

SPECIFICATIONS AND PERFORMANCE (SH-2F)

Manufacturer: Kaman Aircraft Corporation, Bloomfield, Connecticut

Type: Antisubmarine and antiship missile defense helicopter

Accommodation: Pilot, copilot, and one sensor operator

Power plant: Two General Electric T58-GE 8F turboshaft engines of 1,350 shaft hp (1,007 kw) each

Dimensions: Main rotor diameter, 44 ft. (13.41 m); tail rotor diameter, 18 ft. 2 in. (2.49 m); length overall, 52 ft. 7 in. (16.03 m); length, nose section and blades folded, 38 ft. 4 in. (11.68 m); height, 15 ft. 6 in. (4.72 m)

Weights: Empty, 7,040 lb. (3,193 kg); normal takeoff wgt., 12,800 lb. (5,805 kg); max. takeoff wgt., 13,300 lb. (6,033 kg)

Performance: Max. speed, sea level, 165 mph (265 km/h); cruise speed, 150 mph (241 km/h); max. rate of climb, 2,440 ft./min. (744 m); service ceiling, 22,500 ft. (6,860 m); hover ceiling, 15,400 ft. (4,695 m); max. range, 445 miles (716 km)

Armament: One torpedo

Sikorsky SH-60B Seahawk approaches landing pad on frigate *McInerney* in first open sea trials of LAMPS III helicopter. Winds neared 60 mph, with 12-foot waves and ship rolls of 25 degrees.

SIKORSKY SH-60B SEAHAWK

The SH-60B helicopter is scheduled to serve as a vital part of LAMPS Mark III, a newer and more complex ship-air weapons system which promises to revolutionize the role of small surface vessels in defense of the fleet. Thus the Seahawk takes on a significance above and beyond the fact that it is the Navy's newest helicopter.

As an air vehicle of the improved system, the Seahawk will be based aboard escort ships (frigates, destroyers, and cruisers) to help carry out the LAMPS III mission—detecting and destroying hostile submarines and ships. The SH-60B will also be used for such secondary missions as search and rescue, medical evacuation, resupply of ships at sea, and Naval gunfire spotting.

LAMPS III brings to small ships an even greater "over the horizon" range, making them powerful, independent units with their own built-in air strength. Most present-day escort vessels lack aircraft and have only a 20-mile radius of operation for detection and attack, which means they can cover only 1,200 square miles of ocean. With LAMPS III, each ship can expand its defense coverage to over 30,000 square miles. One Seahawk-equipped frigate does the job requiring 20 or more of its predecessors.

The earlier LAMPS ship-air combination is also outstripped by the new system. The LAMPS I helicopter has a 40-mile radius, a one-hour flight duration, and carries one torpedo. The Seahawk of LAMPS III triples the radius and doubles the flight time and torpedo load. Also the earlier system lacks the close tie-in of computers aboard the ships and copters.

As a defender of the fleet, LAMPS III represents an ideal combination of three elements: 1—the surface ship's endurance; 2—the helicopter's speed and versatility; and 3—the miracles of electronic data processing. Computers aboard the helicopter and ship (a "ship system with wings," it has been called) combine to provide a complete picture of potential enemy threats, with the ultimate result being greatly increased sea control.

Each surface vessel will provide a home for two Seahawks. This includes hangar space and facilities for maintenance, launch, recovery, and in-flight (hovering) refueling of the helicopters.

The SH-60B, which first flew on December 12, 1979, is derived from the U.S. Army's UH-60B Blackhawk, a utility tactical helicopter. The Seahawk retains the Blackhawk's rotors, transmission, engines, control systems, and structures. A design feature of both aircraft is their composite main rotor blades which use titanium spars, lightweight honeycomb fillers, and fiber glass skins, a combination that eliminates corrosion—especially important in shipboard operation.

Changes in the Seahawk include automatic rotor blade folding for hangar storage, and a shorter wheelbase for operation from the shipboard helipads. Also LAMPS equipment has been added—surface search radar, magnetic anomaly detection (MAD), sonobuoys, electronic support measures (ESM), torpedo racks, and the latest equipment for all-weather flight.

During 1980 and '81 the SH-60B underwent extensive Navy evaluation, flight testing, and shipboard trials, including the training of pilots and ships' crews in the operation of a system for winching the Seahawk down to shipboard helipads in rough weather.

The LAMPS III program calls for purchase of more than 200 Seahawks at a cost of more than $750 million, with deliveries to the fleet scheduled to begin in 1984.

SPECIFICATIONS AND PERFORMANCE

Manufacturer: Sikorsky Aircraft, a division of United Technologies, Stratford, Connecticut

Type: Ship-based LAMPS III helicopter, chiefly for antisubmarine warfare

Accommodation: Pilot, copilot/airborne tactical officer, and sensor operator

Power plant: Two General Electric T700-GE-401 turboshaft engines of 1,560 shaft hp each (normal operation) and 1,723 shaft hp each (emergency operation)

Dimensions: Overall length, 64 ft. 10 in. (19.76 m); fuselage length, 50 ft. ¾ in. (15.26 m); height, 17 ft. 2 in. (5.23 m); main rotor diameter, 53 ft. 8 in. (16.36 m); tail rotor diameter, 11 ft. (3.35 m)

Weights: Empty, 14,000 lb. (6,350 kg); max. gross wgt., 20,800 lb. (9,435 kg); mission (ASW) takeoff wgt., 20,244 lb. (9,183 kg)

Performance: Max. speed, 178 mph (286 km/h); cruise speed, 149.5 mph (240.5 km/h); vertical rate of climb, 1,192 ft./min. (357.6 m); max. range, 575 miles (925 km); endurance, 5 hours

Armament: Two torpedoes, 25 sonobuoys, 50 "dwarf" sonobuoys

Seahawk sea trials marked first time a new Recovery Assist, Securing, and Traversing (RAST) system (shown here) was used in open ocean.

Part Six / PATROL AIRCRAFT

LOCKHEED P-3 ORION   The four-engine P-3C, the most advanced of the Lockheed Orion series now flying, is regarded by the U.S. Navy as the most effective of its land-based antisubmarine aircraft. Introduced into service in 1969, the P-3C revolutionized ASW surveillance with the installation of an on-board digital computer that integrates the operations of the aircraft's communications, navigation, ASW avionics, flight controls, and weapons systems.

The P-3C traces its origins back to 1957 when the Navy asked the aircraft manufacturers to submit design proposals for a new high-performance antisubmarine patrol aircraft to replace the twin-engine Lockheed P-2V Neptune then in service. The need was for a larger aircraft with higher speed and longer range.

The Navy recommended that, to save time and money, the manufacturers adapt an aircraft already in production rather than submit an entirely new design. Lockheed's turboprop Electra was being produced for the airlines at the time, and it was an adaptation of that commercial transport which, in April, 1958, was selected as winner of the design competition.

Radome containing MAD (Magnetic Anomaly Detector) gear extends from tail of Lockheed P-3C Orion.

Camera shutter speed "stops" propellers of P-3C Orion climbing at 213 mph with props turning at 1,020 rpm.

The Orion retained unchanged the wings, tail assembly, engines, and many other parts of the Electra, but was substantially modified for its military role. Extensive new electronics, a bomb bay for torpedoes, depth bombs, mines, or nuclear weapons, underwing pylons to carry mines or rockets, and a searchlight under the right wing were among the changes made.

The Orion prototype, designated YP-3A, first flew on November 25, 1959. Deliveries of the new patrol plane began in March, 1961, and the P-3 has been in continuous production ever since. By December, 1979, Lockheed had built 500 Orions in five different models, including 157 P-3As, 144 P-3Bs, 190 P-3Cs, six P-3Fs (a version of the C), and three P-3Ds.

The A, B, C, and F models are all antisubmarine aircraft. The D model, designed for airborne research work, was used for a five-year mission to map the earth's magnetic field, a project directed by the U.S. Naval Oceanographic Office. Other D models performed atmospheric research and weather modification experiments. On November 4, 1972, a P-3D flown by the Navy's Oceanographic Development Squadron

8 (VXN-8), based at the Naval Air Test Center, Patuxent River, Maryland, set a world closed-circuit distance record for turboprop aircraft with a flight of 6,278 miles (10,103 kilometers). Other Orions, fitted with special radomes on top and under their fuselages, have been used for weather and electronic reconnaissance, replacing the older Lockheed EC-121 Constellations, piston-powered planes which ended their service with the Navy in the late 1970s.

The bulk of Orion production has gone to the U.S. Navy, but the plane was also chosen by the defense forces of eight other nations and, by 1980, was being flown by six of them.

Continuous equipment improvements have been installed in the P-3C since 1975 and it is expected to remain in production at least until the mid-1980s and to serve as an active U.S. Naval aircraft until the year 2000.

Specifications and Performance (P-3C)

Manufacturer: Lockheed-California Company, a division of Lockheed Corporation, Burbank, California

Type: Four-turboprop, land-based, antisubmarine aircraft

Accommodation: Ten-man crew. (Main cabin has five-man tactical section with latest electronic, magnetic, and sonic detection equipment, plus galley and crew rest area.)

Power plant: Four Allison T56-A-14 turboprop engines of 4,910 shaft hp (3,661 kw) each, driving four Hamilton Standard 4-blade constant-speed propellers

Dimensions: Span, 99 ft. 8 in. (30.37 m); length overall, 116 ft. 10 in. (35.61 m); height, 33 ft. 8½ in. (10.29 m); propeller diameter, 13 ft. 6 in. (4.11 m); wing area, 1,300 sq. ft. (120.77 sq. m)

Weights: Empty, 61,491 lb. (27,890 kg); max. normal takeoff wgt., 135,000 lb. (61,235 kg); max. permissible wgt., 142,000 lb. (64,410 kg); max. landing wgt., 103,880 lb. (47,119 kg)

Performance: Max. speed, 473 mph (761 km/h); cruise speed, 378 mph (608 km/h); patrol speed, 237 mph (381 km/h); stalling speed, flaps down, 129 mph (208 km/h); max. rate of climb, 1,950 ft./min. (594 m); service ceiling, 28,300 ft. (8,625 m); takeoff run, 4,240 ft. (1,290 m); max. mission radius, 2,383 miles (3,835 km)

Armament: In bomb bay: various combinations of mines, depth bombs, and torpedoes, or 2 nuclear depth bombs and 4 torpedoes. On ten underwing pylons: various combinations of mines, rockets, and torpedoes. Max. total weapons load carried internally, 7,252 lb. (3,290 kg); max. total weapons load carried externally, 12,000 lb. (5,443 kg)

Part Seven / TRANSPORT AIRCRAFT

BEECHCRAFT UC-12B   The latest of three types of Beech aircraft used by the U.S. Navy is the UC-12B, a military version of the 14-place Beechcraft Super King Air Model 200. The UC-12B is also the latest member of the Beechcraft King Air family of turboprop aircraft, the most widely used of their type in the world.

First delivered in September, 1979, to the Naval Air Station, New Orleans, Louisiana, the UC-12Bs were scheduled to be stationed at 30 Naval sites worldwide during the ensuing three years. The aircraft are used for a variety of transport, utility, and training missions in support of both the active Naval forces and the Naval Reserve. Typical tasks include rapid transportation of repair crews, accident investigation teams, high priority equipment, inspection and technical teams, and medical evacuation of ill or injured personnel. Scheduling of these operations in the U.S. is coordinated through the Naval Air Logistics Center in New Orleans.

The UC-12B has been described as "one of the most versatile airplanes ever designed," a superlative that seems to be supported by the following: the UC-12B's short takeoff and landing runs enable it to operate from small, unimproved fields, or grassy runways; ability to cruise at over 300 miles an hour at

The Beech UC-12B is a military version of the commercial Super King Air.

altitudes above 30,000 feet, and fly nonstop for more than 1,700 miles. Its modern avionics systems give it all-weather operation anywhere in the world.

The UC-12B's quick-change interior, large cargo door, oversize tires for soft-field operations, and an undercarriage strengthened for high-impact landings provide rapid and safe transportation of VIP passengers and top-priority cargo. Reversing propellers reduces landing distances while increasing the life of tires and brakes. Dual controls permit two-pilot operation or flight crew training. The pressurized and air-conditioned cabin seats up to eight passengers.

The UC-12B is essentially the same as the C-12A previously built for the U.S. Army and Air Force. The principal differences are newer model turboprop engines which increase the horsepower per engine from 750 to 850, a larger cargo door, and strengthened landing gear for unimproved airstrips.

The Navy is buying more than 60 UC-12Bs, with deliveries scheduled to run through April, 1982. The new planes will replace about 130 aging piston-powered aircraft and supplement the Navy's big C-9 (DC-9) jet transports.

With acquisition of the UC-12B, the Navy now has three Beechcraft types in its fleet, the others being the single-turbine T-34C and twin-turbine T-44A trainers (both described in Part Nine/Trainer Aircraft). The UC-12B is also going to the U.S. Marine Corps, which adds up to all four U.S. military services now flying the Super King Air type aircraft.

SPECIFICATIONS AND PERFORMANCE

Manufacturer: Beech Aircraft Corporation, Wichita, Kansas

Type: Twin turboprop personnel-utility transport

Accommodation: Pilot, copilot, and eight passengers or cargo

Power plant: Two Pratt & Whitney Aircraft of Canada PT6A-41 turboprop engines of 850 shaft hp each, driving 3-blade, full-feathering, reversible propellers

Dimensions: Span, 54 ft. 6 in. (16.35 m); length, 43 ft. 9 in. (13.13 m); height, 14 ft. 6 in. (4.35 m); cabin length, 16 ft. 8 in. (4.98 m)

Weights: Empty, 7,869 lb. (3,569 kg); max. takeoff and landing wgt., 12,500 lb. (5,670 kg)

Performance: Max. cruise speed, 310 mph (499 km/h); rate of climb, 2,320 ft./min. (696 m); service ceiling, 31,000 ft. (9,300 m); range, 1,760 miles (2,832 km); stall speed, flaps down, 92 mph (148 km/h)

Armament: None

As a COD aircraft, Grumman C-2A Greyhound provides key link between aircraft carriers and shore bases.

GRUMMAN C-2A GREYHOUND

Soon after the E-2 Hawkeye program was started in 1956 Grumman Aerospace Corporation submitted a proposal to the Navy for a transport derivative of the new early warning aircraft.

This action led to an order from the Navy for three prototypes of the transport which was given the designation C-2A and later the name Greyhound.

The C-2A used the same wings, tail section, and power plant of the E-2A Hawkeye, but had a new fuselage with a rear loading ramp and arrangements for carrying as many as 39 passengers, various types of cargoes, or, as an ambulance, 20 stretchers.

The Greyhound's chief job is carrier-on-board delivery (COD), making it a vital personnel and supply link between aircraft carriers and shore bases. The first of the prototypes flew on November 18, 1964, and production began in 1965. The first production aircraft were delivered to Fleet Tactical Support Squadron 50 (VRC-50) which first put the Greyhound into operation in December, 1966.

Greyhound carries 39 passengers, is a transport derivative of the Grumman E-2 Hawkeye early warning aircraft.

SPECIFICATIONS AND PERFORMANCE

Manufacturer: Grumman Aerospace Corporation, Bethpage, New York

Type: Carrier-on-board delivery transport

Accommodation: Crew of three or four, 39 passengers

Power plant: Two Allison T56-A-425 turboprop engines of 4,910 hp (3,661 kw) each; two 4-blade Hamilton Standard propellers, foam-filled and with steel spar and fiber glass shells

Dimensions: Span, 80 ft. 7 in. (24.56 m); length, 56 ft. 7 in. (16.9 m); height, 15 ft. 11 in. (4.8 m); wing area, 700 sq. ft. (65.03 sq. m)

Weights: Empty, 31,250 lb. (14,175 kg); max. gross wgt., 54,382 lb. (24,668 kg)

Performance: Max. speed, 352 mph (566 km/h); cruise speed, 296 mph (476 km/h); initial climb, 2,330 ft./min. (700 m); service ceiling, 28,800 ft. (8,650 m); range, 1,655 miles (2,663 km)

Armament: None

GRUMMAN C-1A TRADER   An earlier and smaller COD aircraft is the C-1A Trader, which appeared in 1955 as a derivative of the Grumman S-2 Tracker, an antisubmarine aircraft which had its origins in the early 1950s.

Like the Tracker, the Trader is a high-wing monoplane powered by two piston engines. The transport version, however, was given a new fuselage with room for nine passengers, mail, and cargo. Like the later Greyhounds, the Traders are operated from aircraft carriers, making use of the same catapult equipment that launches the carriers' fighters and bombers.

C-1A production totalled 89, including four which were modified as EC-1As by installing equipment for electronic countermeasures missions. Also derived from the C-1A was the EC-1B whose major external changes were a massive dishlike radome mounted above the fuselage, and a new tail unit with twin fins and rudders and a central fin, replacing the single fin and rudder of the C-1A.

Piston-powered Grumman C-1A Trader is an earlier, smaller COD aircraft.

C-1A Trader is derived from Grumman's S-2 Tracker, an antisubmarine aircraft of the 1950s.

SPECIFICATIONS AND PERFORMANCE

Manufacturer: Grumman Aircraft Engineering Corporation, Bethpage, New York

Type: Carrier-on-board delivery transport

Accommodation: Two pilots, nine passengers, mail, cargo

Power plant: Two Wright R-1820-82WA piston engines of 1,525 hp each

Dimensions: Span, 72 ft. 7 in. (21.7 m); length, 43 ft. 6 in. (13 m); height, 16 ft. 7 in. (4.9 m); wing area, 499 sq. ft. (46.4 sq. m)

Weights: Empty, 19,000 lb. (8,600 kg); gross wgt. (approx.), 27,000 lb. (12,250 kg)

Performance: Max. speed, 253 mph (407 km/h); cruise speed, 149 mph (240 km/h); initial climb, 1,800 ft./min. (540 m); service ceiling, 22,000 ft. (6,600 m); range, 1,150 miles (1,850 km)

Armament: None

LOCKHEED C-130 HERCULES   No aircraft better exemplifies the worldwide scope of U.S. Naval Aviation than the Lockheed C-130 Hercules, a turboprop transport which, with its 132-foot wingspan and massive cargo-carrying fuselage, is the Navy's largest airplane.

U.S. Navy Hercules transports served several different missions, one of the most notable being their years of assistance in advancing peacetime scientific knowledge, especially in the Antarctic. The year 1981 marked the 25th anniversary of the Navy's VXE-6 squadron which for many years has operated ski-equipped LC-130 Hercules transports out of McMurdo Sound in Antarctica to resupply fifteen National Science Foundation research stations across the five-and-a-half-million square mile white continent.

The squadron, whose home base is at Point Mugu, California, flies its six Hercules as the major support transport aircraft in Antarctica throughout the continent's summer months, October through February. The planes are owned by the National Science Foundation and operated by the Navy as a vital aid for a fifteen-nation international research program known as Operation Deep Freeze. During the five-

Largest airplane ever to fly from a carrier, a Lockheed KC-130F Hercules takes off from canted flight deck.

Ski-equipped Lockheed C-130 Hercules transports serve in the Antarctic as part of annual Operation Deep Freeze.

month season they fly some 10 million pounds of cargo from Christchurch, New Zealand, to the fifteen stations. It is a grueling assignment. One Hercules remained frozen for a year on a two-mile-high ice plateau after striking a series of two-foot-high ice waves on an unsuccessful takeoff. The plane was rescued in minus-50 degree (F) temperatures by a Lockheed/Navy repair team in what the National Science Foundation described as "a major feat in aviation and Antarctic history."

The LC-130 is the largest ski-equipped aircraft in the world. Each of its aluminum main skis weighs one ton. The landing gear is a unique "ski-and-wheel" system which enables the big transport to take off from land with wheels or skis.

The Hercules is the largest and heaviest aircraft ever to operate from an aircraft carrier. In tests aboard the U.S.S. *Forrestal* in 1963 a U.S. Marine Corps KC-130F refueler/transport, flown by Navy pilots from the Naval Air Test Center, Patuxent River, Maryland, made 21 landings (without using tail hook arresting gear) and 21 takeoffs (without catapult or jet assist). The landings (made possible by the plane's four reversible propellers) ranged in distance from 270 feet (at 85,000 pounds gross weight) to 460 feet (at 121,000 pounds).

The Hercules, originally designed in 1951 to meet U.S. Air Force requirements, made its first flight on August 23, 1954. The Navy became interested in the Hercules in 1960 when the Air Force demonstrated the plane's potential for Arctic and Antarctic operations, using five C-130s in Operation Deep Freeze

The year 1981 marked 25th anniversary of Navy Squadron VXE-6, known as "Penguin Airlines," which flies Hercules transports from New Zealand to 15 research stations in Antarctic.

1960. The big transport proved so useful that the Navy bought four C-130s for operation by squadron VXE-6 in Deep Freeze 1961 and in many subsequent scientific operations in the Antarctic.

Meanwhile the Marine Corps became interested in the Hercules as an aerial tanker, ordering 46 planes which were designated KC-130F. (It was one of these which made the historic takeoffs and landings aboard the carrier *Forrestal*.) The Navy later bought seven Hercules transports, similar to the Marines' tankers but with the refueling equipment removed. These were designated as C-130Fs. Another specialized role for the Navy Hercules was that of communications relay in support of worldwide operations of Fleet Ballistic Missile submarines—the EC-130Q described in Part Four/Reconnaissance Aircraft. Versions of the Hercules were also bought through the Navy for the U.S. Coast Guard for air-sea rescue work.

In all, approximately 120 Hercules type aircraft have been bought by the Navy, Marine Corps, and Coast Guard—roughly 7 percent of Lockheed's total Hercules output. A relatively modest number, yet their impact has been far-ranging, diverse, and often dramatic.

SPECIFICATIONS AND PERFORMANCE (KC-130F)

Manufacturer: Lockheed-Georgia Company, Marietta, Georgia

Type: In-flight refueling tanker and transport

Accommodation: Crew of seven as a tanker; crew of five as a transport; up to 92 troops or 74 stretchers

Power plant: Four Allison T56-A-16 turboprop engines of 4,910 shaft hp each

Dimensions: Span, 132 ft. 7 in. (39.7 m); length, 97 ft. 8 in. (29.3 m); height, 38 ft. 3½ in. (11.5 m); wing area, 1,745 sq. ft. (162 sq. m)

Weights: Wgt. empty, tanker, 74,454 lb. (33,772 kg); wgt. empty, transport, 70,491 lb. (31,975 kg); max. takeoff wgt., 135,000 lb. (61,236 kg)

Performance: Max. cruise speed, 357 mph (574 km/h); long-range cruise speed, 343 mph (552 km/h); refueling speed, 250 mph (402 km/h); range with full payload, up to 3,000 miles (4,827 km)

Armament: None

BOEING VERTOL H-46 SEA KNIGHT
The H-46 Sea Knight is a military version of the Boeing Vertol model 107-II, a twin-turbine medium transport helicopter used for both military and civilian operations in the United States, Canada, Sweden, and Japan. Its principal feature is its tandem main

Ship-to-ship transfer of supplies is one of the many jobs done by Boeing Vertol UH-46 Sea Knight helicopters.

Sea Knight lifts cargo from a supply vessel to an aircraft carrier at sea.

rotor design. Production was concentrated chiefly from 1964–71 when more than 600 Sea Knights were built. Production continues at Kawasaki Heavy Industries, Ltd., in Japan under a license arrangement with Boeing Vertol.

The Sea Knight is essentially a U.S. Marine Corps assault transport designated CH-46 and designed to operate from Navy carriers as well as from shore bases. Its mission is transportation of troops, fuel, and supplies.

Boeing's Vertol Division won a design competition in 1961 for a new assault transport for the Marine

Corps, the winner being designated CH-46A. The principal differences between the CH-46A and the commercial 107-II were increased engine power, folding rotor blades for carrier deck storage, and a built-in cargo loading system. Its mission was to carry 4,000 pounds of cargo (or up to 17 fully equipped troops) over a combat radius of 115 miles at a speed of 150 miles an hour. Rapid loading and unloading of troops and cargo was a prime requirement.

The CH-46A first flew on October 16, 1962. Production contracts followed, with the later D and E models having greater power and improved avionics and instrument panels. In 1946 the Navy purchased a specialized version of the Sea Knight, the UH-46A, for its Vertical Replenishment Program—the transfer of supplies from supply ships to combat vessels at sea. Another Navy version, the HH-46, is used for shore-based search and rescue. In all, Navy and Marine Corps purchase of Sea Knights totaled 624 by the end of 1970.

The Sea Knights are now undergoing modification and modernization programs. Included are further increases in engine power, crash-resistant seats for pilot and copilot, combat-resistant fuel system, and an improved rescue system. Boeing Vertol is also producing fiber glass rotor blades to replace the metal blades in the CH-46 fleet. Together, these programs are expected to keep the Sea Knight in service well into the 1980s.

SPECIFICATIONS AND PERFORMANCE (CH-46D)

Manufacturer: Boeing Vertol Company, a division of the Boeing Company, Morton, Pennsylvania

Type: Combat assault helicopter (Marines); ship-to-ship supply transport (Navy)

Accommodation: Pilot, copilot, plane captain; up to 17 troops or 15 stretchers with two attendants; or 25 passengers.

Power plant: Two General Electric T58-GE-10 shaft turbine engines of 1,400 shaft hp each

Dimensions: Rotor diameter, 51 ft. (15.3 m) each; fuselage length, 44 ft. 10 in. (13.5 m); length overall, including rotor blades, 84 ft. 4 in. (25.3 m); height, 16 ft. 8 in. (5 m)

Weights: Empty, 13,065 lb. (5.926 kg); gross wgt., 23,000 lb. (10,433 kg)

Performance: Max. speed, sea level, 166 mph (267 km/h); cruise speed, 154 mph (247.8 km/h); initial climb, 1,715 ft./min. (515 m); service ceiling, 14,000 ft. (4,200 m); range, 230 miles (370 km)

Armament: None

Twin-turbine Bell UH-1N Iroquois is used as a local base transport and also to support annual Operation Deep Freeze in Antarctica.

BELL UH-1 IROQUOIS   For two decades the Navy has operated various versions of one of the world's most widely used turbine-powered helicopters, the Bell UH-1 Iroquois series. Civil and military missions for the popular UH-1 include personnel and cargo transport, medical evacuation, rescue, reconnaissance, and weapons platform.

The Navy's initial purchase of the Iroquois was in behalf of the Marine Corps which in 1962 required an assault combat helicopter to support its shore-based and amphibious attack operations. Chosen to meet this requirement was the single-turbine UH-1E which was similar in most respects to the U.S. Army's combat-proven UH-1B Huey, a military version of Bell's commercial model 204.

Deliveries of the UH-1E to the Marines began in early 1964 with a total of 250 being received, plus 20 TH-1Es for the training of crews. (In 1968 the Navy purchased two other versions of the Iroquois to meet

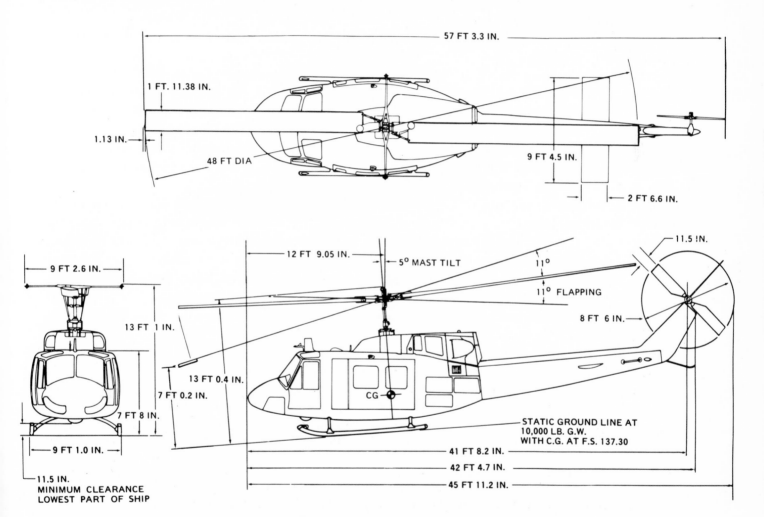

57 FT 3.3 IN.

1 FT. 11.38 IN.

1.13 IN.

48 FT DIA

9 FT 4.5 IN.

2 FT 6.6 IN.

9 FT 2.6 IN.

13 FT 1 IN.

13 FT 0.4 IN.

7 FT 0.2 IN.

7 FT 8 IN.

9 FT 1.0 IN.

11.5 IN.
MINIMUM CLEARANCE
LOWEST PART OF SHIP

12 FT 9.05 IN.

5° MAST TILT

11°

11° FLAPPING

11.5 IN.

8 FT 6 IN.

CG

STATIC GROUND LINE AT
10,000 LB. G.W.
WITH C.G. AT F.S. 137.30

41 FT 8.2 IN.

42 FT 4.7 IN.

45 FT 11.2 IN.

Drawings show details and dimensions of Bell UH-1N helicopter.

its needs for rescue and training helicopters. These will be discussed under Rescue Aircraft and Trainer Aircraft, respectively.)

The most significant Navy connection with the Iroquois type helicopter came in 1968 with the purchase of the UH-1N (Bell model 212), a twin-engine version of the Bell 204. The new helicopter featured a "TwinPac" power plant consisting of two turboshaft engines joined to a common gearbox, an arrangement which provided increased power along with twin-engine reliability.

The UH-1N, which was also purchased by the U.S. Air Force, became a major procurement program for the Navy and Marine Corps. Deliveries began in 1971 and continued throughout the 1970s to meet the plan of over 250 aircraft required by the Navy and Marine Corps.

The Navy employs the UH-1N chiefly as a local base transport at Naval air stations and also to support the annual Deep Freeze operations in the Antarctic. The Marines have found a variety of uses for their UH-1Ns: troop transport, command posts, amphibious assault, cargo and equipment transport, medical evacuation, combat reconnaissance support, and counterinsurgency operations.

The 15-place UH-1N has the same seating and stretcher arrangements as the Army's single-engine Huey, but its twin-turbine power plant assures greater safety in poor weather, on hot days, and at high altitudes. A Bell automatic flight control system (AFCS) also increases safety while easing the workload on the pilot.

SPECIFICATIONS AND PERFORMANCE (UH-1N)

Manufacturer: Bell Helicopter Textron, a division of Textron, Inc., Fort Worth, Texas

Type: Personnel and cargo transport helicopter

Accommodation: Pilot, copilot, crew chief, and 12 passengers

Power plant: United Aircraft of Canada T400-CP-400 twin turboshaft (TwinPac) engines of 1,800 total shaft hp (max. for takeoff), and 1,530 shaft hp (max. for cruising)

Dimensions: Overall length, 57 ft. (17.1 m); fuselage length, 43 ft. (12.9 m); overall height, 14 ft. 5 in. (4.3 m); main rotor diameter, 48 ft. (14.4 m)

Weights: Empty, 5,936 lb. (2.693 kg); max. gross wgt., 10,500 lb. (4,763 kg); max. payload plus fuel, 4,222 lb. (1,915 kg)

Performance: Max. speed, 126.5 mph (203.5 km/h); service ceiling, 16,500 ft. (4,950 m); max. rate of climb, 1,310 ft./min. (393 m); max. range, 282 miles (453 m)

Armament: None

MCDONNELL DOUGLAS C-9B SKYTRAIN II   The Navy's C-9B Skytrain II is a military adaptation of the widely used McDonnell Douglas DC-9 commercial transport. A special convertible passenger/cargo aircraft, the C-9B is named after the Navy's "old reliable," the R4D Skytrain which was derived from the venerable Douglas DC-3, first built in the mid-1930s. The Skytrain II's top cruise speed of over 570 miles an hour makes it the Navy's fastest transport.

The C-9B is a sweptwing jet with its two turbofan engines mounted in pods on each side of the rear fuselage. As a cargo aircraft it can carry a load of over 32,000 pounds on eight standard military pallets which are loaded through a cargo door at the port forward end of the cabin. As a personnel transport it has space for 90 passengers or, in a "high density" seating arrangement, as many as 107. In a combined

Navy's fastest transport is the Douglas C-9B Skytrain II, military version of the widely used DC-9 airliner.

Sweptwing C-9B carries as many as 107 passengers or 16 tons of cargo at cruise speeds as high as 570 mph.

passenger/cargo configuration it carries its cargo on three pallets in the forward cabin area, with 45 passengers in the rear section.

Passengers enter and leave the aircraft on stairs at the left forward side of the cabin and beneath the aft section of the fuselage. The stairs are hydraulically operated from inside the cabin to make the C-9B independent of ground facilities. To complete this independence, an auxiliary power unit provides both electrical and hydraulic services when the aircraft is on the ground. Air conditioning and pressurization give the cabin sea level conditions up to an altitude of 18,500 feet, and 8,000-foot altitude conditions up to 35,000 feet.

The Navy ordered eight Skytrain IIs in 1972 and six more in 1974. The first of these made its initial flight on February 7, 1973, and the first deliveries came in May of that year.

106

Manufacturer: Douglas Aircraft Company, a division of McDonnell Douglas Corporation, Long Beach, California

Type: Fleet logistic support transport

Accommodation: Pilot, copilot, crew chief, two cabin attendants, and up to 107 passengers

Power plant: Two Pratt & Whitney JT8D-9 turbofan engines of 14,500 lb. (6,577 kg) thrust each

Dimensions: Span, 93 ft. 5 in. (28.47 m); length, 119 ft. 3½ in. (36.37 m); height, 27 ft. 6 in. (8.38 m)

Weights: Empty (passenger), 65,283 lb. (29,612 kg); empty (cargo), 59,706 lb. (27,082 kg); max. payload, 31,125 lb. (14,118 kg); max. takeoff wgt., 110,000 lb. (49,900 kg); max. landing wgt., 99,000 lb. (44,906 kg)

Performance: Max. cruise speed, 576 mph (927 km/h); long-range cruise speed, 504 mph (811 km/h); landing distance, 2,580 ft. (786 m); range, with 10,000 lb. (4,535 kg) payload, 2,923 miles (4,704 km)

Armament: None

SIKORSKY CH-53E SUPER STALLION

The largest and most powerful helicopter in the Western world, the triple-turbine CH-53E Super Stallion is a growth version of the twin-turbine H-53 Sea Stallion which, in its various versions, has served the Navy and Marine Corps since 1965.

With its massive bulk and awkwardly tilted tail pylon, the Super Stallion is built not for beauty but for performance. It has, for example, 100 percent greater lift than the earlier CH-53D with only a 50 percent increase in power. The CH-53E carries a 16-ton external load (on its cargo hook) over a radius of 57 miles, even under the adverse conditions of 90 degree (F) temperatures, and up to 18 tons over shorter distances.

The Super Stallion's additional lift is achieved by harnessing its increased engine power to seven main rotor blades of lightweight, strong, composite materials. (The CH-53D has six aluminum main blades.) Also, the new blades are wider and the rotor diameter is increased from 72 to 79 feet.

The Super Stallion can carry up to 55 troops at speeds as high as 195 miles an hour. It is the largest helicopter capable of operating from or being based aboard the Navy's present and planned ships, an important factor for the future. Vital also is the CH-53E's new automatic flight control system (AFCS), one of the most advanced in the helicopter industry. The flight control system, built by Hamilton Standard Division of United Technologies, uses two digital on-board computers to hold the helicopter in whatever flight attitude desired. The unit is 42 percent lighter, 50 percent smaller, requires 41 percent less

Three turbine engines of huge Sikorsky CH-53E Super Stallion develop a total of more than 13,000 horsepower, drive a seven-blade main rotor 79 feet in diameter.

power and, according to Sikorsky, has proved to be 900 percent more reliable than the systems used in the earlier Sea Stallions.

The prototype YCH-53E made its first flight on March 1, 1974, and the initial production model first flew on December 13, 1980. Further flight testing of the first production CH-53E followed at the Naval Air Test Center, Patuxent River, Maryland, with deliveries to the fleet starting in mid-1981.

Future plans call for the Department of Defense to purchase 49 Super Stallions, valued at more than $750 million, with the Navy receiving 16 and the Marines 33. Navy missions include ship-to-ship and ship-to-shore logistics, support of mobile construction battalions, and airborne minesweeping. The CH-53E has powered blade folding and tail pylon folding systems for easy storage aboard ships.

Ninety-three percent of Marine Corps equipment is transportable by the CH-53E. In one lift it can deliver the new MI98 155-mm howitzer, ammunition, and crew. Within its huge cargo cabin it can transport support equipment for an entire squadron of the Marines' Harrier vertical takeoff fighters. In-flight refueling gives it unlimited range.

SPECIFICATIONS AND PERFORMANCE

Manufacturer: Sikorsky Aircraft, a division of United Technologies, Stratford, Connecticut

Type: Heavy duty, multipurpose helicopter, shore- or carrier-based

Accommodation: Pilot, copilot, crew chief, up to 55 troops

Power plant: Three General Electric T64-GE-415 turboshaft engines of 4,380 shaft hp (3,266 kw) max. rating each; normal continuous power, 3,670 shaft hp (2,737 kw) each

Dimensions: Main rotor diameter, 79 ft. (24.08 m); tail rotor diameter, 20 ft. (6.1 m); length overall, 99 ft. 1 in. (30.2 m); height overall, 28 ft. 5 in. (8.66 m)

Weights: Empty, 32,878 lb. (14,910 kg); external payload for 57.7 miles (92.5 km) radius, 32,200 lb. (14,605 kg); internal payload for 115 miles (185 km) radius, 30,000 lb. (13,607 kg); max. takeoff wgt., 69,750 lb. (31,638 kg)

Performance: Max. speed, 196 mph (315 km/h); cruise speed, 173 mph (278 km/h); max. rate of climb, 2,750 ft./min. (825 m); hover ceiling, 9,500 ft. (2,898 m); service ceiling, 18,500 ft. (5,643 m); max. range, 1,288 miles (2,076 km)

Armament: None

Part Eight / RESCUE AIRCRAFT

It was almost forty years ago that the Navy discovered the helicopter's usefulness as a rescue vehicle, a discovery that since has led to the saving of countless lives.

On January 3, 1944, when the U.S. destroyer *Turner* exploded off the New Jersey shore, Coast Guard Commander Frank Erickson braved snow and sleet to fly a little R-4 helicopter from the tip of Manhattan to the beach at Sandy Hook, New Jersey, speeding a cargo of life-saving blood plasma to 100 badly burned survivors.

Three years later, on February 9, 1947, Dmitri (Jimmy) Viner, a Sikorsky test pilot, picked a Navy pilot from the ocean after the flier's Helldiver had ditched during a landing approach. The pickup was one of four such rescues made during a two-week helicopter demonstration aboard Navy carriers in the Atlantic—achievements which won Viner a Navy "Very well done" and the helicopter a permanent place in Naval Aviation.

The Naval aircraft assigned to rescue work today were not designed specifically for rescue but are adaptations of helicopters widely used for other duties, chiefly antisubmarine warfare and general utility. They include the Kaman HH-2D Seasprite, Sikorsky HH-3A Sea King, Boeing Vertol HH-46A Sea Knight, and Bell HH-1K Iroquois. In most cases their appearance, specifications, and performance are practically identical with their namesakes described earlier in this book.

KAMAN HH-2 SEASPRITE   When the Seasprites proved valuable for rescue missions in Vietnam, six of the early single-engine models were converted to an armed HH-2C configuration with two engines. The changes included installing a 7.62-mm minigun in the nose, two more at the mid-fuselage positions, and the use of armor plate for protection during the dangerous rescue operations which usually required hovering at low altitudes within easy range of gunfire from the ground.

Later about 70 more of the early Seasprites were converted to the twin-engine version under the rescue designation HH-2D. This model and the SH-2F LAMPS I are the only Seasprites now in Naval service. (See Kaman SH-2 Seasprite in the Search Aircraft section for specifications and performance and further details.)

SIKORSKY HH-3A SEA KING   The HH-3A is one of several modifications of the original SH-3A antisubmarine helicopter. The HH-3A conversion was tested in the late 1960s by the Navy as a search-and-rescue aircraft, with armament, armor, and a high-speed rescue hoist. Conversion kits were later sent from Sikorsky to the Navy's overhaul and repair base at Quonset Point, Rhode Island, where 12 conversions were performed. The HH-3As were intended as combat area rescue vehicles and saw service in Vietnam.

The HH-3As included these changes: installation of two electrically powered miniguns in the fuselage, greater engine power, a high-speed refueling and fuel dumping system, a high-speed rescue hoist, modified

Twin-turbine Kaman HH-2D Seasprite was converted to its rescue configuration from earlier single-engine SH-2 models which had been used for antisubmarine and antiship missile defense.

Rescue version of the Sikorsky SH-3 Sea King series is this HH-3A which has several added features, including refueling hoist, fuel dumping system, and long-range fuel tanks.

electronics, external fuel tanks for increased range, and complete armor protection. A reinforced cabin floor was substituted for the sonar opening, or well, used in the SH-3As for ASW missions. Many of the features introduced in the rescue models were used later in the newer antisubmarine Sea Kings—the SH-3G and SH-3H. (See Sikorsky SH-3 Sea King in the Search Aircraft section for specifications and performance and other details.)

BOEING VERTOL HH-46A SEA KNIGHT   The various versions of the Sea Knight have been used chiefly as assault transports for carrying troops, fuel, and supplies (by the Marines as the CH-46) and for general utility such as the transfer of supplies between ships at sea (by the Navy as the UH-46). The Sea Knight has seen only minimal use for rescue work, chiefly for shore-based search and rescue, under the designation HH-46. (See Boeing Vertol H-46 Sea Knight in the Transport section for specifications and performance and other details.)

112

BELL HH-1K IROQUOIS During 1969 and '70 the Navy acquired two new versions of the combat-proven UH-1E, the single-engine assault transport flown by the Marines in Vietnam. The new versions were the HH-1K rescue helicopter and the TH-1L trainer.

The 27 HH-1Ks which were purchased were similar to the UH-1E except that they had greater engine power, different avionics, and the overall bright orange finish which conformed to international practice for rescue aircraft. The HH-1K is one of five different Bell helicopter types still in service with the Navy, principally for utility, training, and rescue operations. (Specifications and performance figures for the twin-engine Bell UH-1N which appear in the Transport section do not apply to the single-engine HH-1K.)

SPECIFICATIONS AND PERFORMANCE (HH-1K)

Manufacturer: Bell Helicopter Textron, a division of Textron, Inc., Fort Worth, Texas

Type: Search-and-rescue helicopter

Accommodation: Pilot, copilot, crew chief, and space for several passengers or stretchers, depending on circumstances

Power plant: One Lycoming T-53-L-13 turboshaft engine of 1,250 shaft hp

Dimensions: Length, 42 ft. 7 in. (12.7 m); rotor diameter, 44 ft. (13.2 m); height, 12 ft. 8 in. (3.78 m); tail rotor diameter, 8 ft. 6 in. (2.55 m)

Weights: Operating wgt., 5,560 lb. (2,522 kg); mission fuel, 1,300 lb. (590 kg); max. gross wgt., 9,500 lb. (4,309 kg)

Performance: Max. speed, 126 mph (203 km/h); max. rate of climb, 1,600 ft./min. (480 m); max. range, 288 miles (464 km); service ceiling, 12,600 ft. (3,780 m)

Armament: None

The HH designation of the foregoing helicopters does not give them an exclusive right to rescue flights, since all helicopters are, by their nature, potential rescue craft. Other Navy copters are often pressed into service in emergencies or for such special assignments as the recovery of astronauts from the sea. Floods, fires, storms, and earthquakes usually leave such isolation and chaos that only helicopters can deliver the necessary food and medical assistance in time to save lives. For many years it has been widely accepted that, worldwide, helicopters have saved "more than 100,000 lives." Today the true figure almost certainly exceeds that estimate, with U.S. Naval helicopters accounting for their full share of the total.

Part Nine / TRAINER AIRCRAFT

BEECHCRAFT T-34 MENTOR   The turbine-powered T-34C proves the wisdom of improving a successful design to meet changing conditions and requirements quickly and at the lowest cost.

The Mentor first appeared in 1953 as an adaptation of the Beechcraft civilian Model 45. The T-34A was ordered that year by the U.S. Air Force as a piston-powered primary trainer, and by the Navy a year later as the T-34B. The Air Force purchased 450 A models through the years and the Navy 423 of the B version.

Experience showed the Mentor to be such a reliable and rugged trainer that in 1973 the Navy asked Beech to modify two T-34Bs with turbine engines and new electronic equipment. The goals were to learn

Beech T-34C Mentor has an outstanding record for ruggedness and reliability as a Navy primary trainer.

whether the Mentor could be upgraded and continue in the training program and, if so, to provide students with the experience of flying turbine-powered planes from the start of their flight training.

The first of the two modified aircraft flew for the first time on September 21, 1973. It was fitted with a 400-horsepower PT-6A engine, a turbine power plant normally rated at 715 horsepower but which was limited (or derated) for the Mentor to provide longer engine life. The T-34C had a gross weight of 1,000 pounds more than that of the T-34B, along with a strengthened fuselage and tail unit to handle the increase.

Beech delivered the first of 116 T-34Cs to the Navy in November, 1977. Naval students began flying the new Mentor in January, 1978, at the Naval Air Station, Whiting Field, Milton, Florida. Through June of 1979 the T-34Cs accumulated over 110,000 hours of flying in student training and established an outstanding record for reliability, maintaining an operational readiness rate of over 92 percent. As a result the Navy ordered an additional quantity of T-34Cs in July, 1979, with deliveries running from November of the following year through April, 1981. This brought the Navy's purchase of T-34Cs to a total of 184 aircraft.

With flying qualities, engine response, and instrumentation similar to those of most small jet aircraft, the T-34C prepares students for the challenge of pure jet flying which awaits them in their more advanced training.

SPECIFICATIONS AND PERFORMANCE

Manufacturer: Beech Aircraft Corporation, Wichita, Kansas

Type: Turbine-powered primary training aircraft

Accommodation: Instructor and student in tandem

Power plant: One Pratt & Whitney of Canada PT6A-25 turboprop engine limited to 400 shaft hp (298 kw), driving a 3-blade metal Hartzell propeller

Dimensions: Span, 33 ft. 4 in. (10.16 m); length, 28 ft. 8 in. (8.75 m); height, 9 ft. 11 in. (3.02 m)

Weights: Empty, 2,940 lb. (1,334 kg); max. gross wgt. 4,300 lb. (1,950 kg)

Performance: Max. level speed, 257 mph (414 km/h); max. cruise speed, 247 mph (397 km/h); stalling speed, flaps up, 63.3 mph (102 km/h); service ceiling, over 30,000 ft. (9,145 m); max. rate of climb, 1,440 ft./min. (432 m); range, 816.5 miles (1,314 km)

Armament: None

Twin-turbine T-44A advanced trainer is an adaptation of the widely used King Air Model 90.

BEECHCRAFT T-44A KING AIR   Another successful adaptation of a civilian aircraft to the requirements of the Naval Air Training Command is the twin-turboprop T-44A advanced trainer.

In 1976 the Beech Aircraft Corporation entered a military version of its widely used Beechcraft King Air Model 90 in an industry competition to provide a new multiengine advanced trainer for the Navy. To avoid development costs, the competition called for "off-the-shelf" aircraft—those already in production. The King Air 90, with a background at that time of 1,100 built and more than four million flight hours logged, won the competition and an initial order for 15 aircraft was placed.

The spring and summer of 1977 found the new T-44As logging 700 flying hours during a three-month program of instructor training and check-out. More importantly, during that period the new trainers achieved an operational readiness ratio (percentage of time available for flight) of 97 percent. This performance enabled the Navy to complete the instructor training phase earlier than expected, to fly 60 percent more training missions than planned, and to begin advance student training at the Naval Air Station, Corpus Christi, Texas, on July 1, a month ahead of the scheduled date.

Deliveries of the new trainer continued during 1978 and '79 and were completed in mid-1980 with a total of 61 T-44As in service. At that point more than 1,500 King Air 90s had been delivered to commercial and military operators in the U.S. and overseas.

The T-44A is designed for a service life of 12,000 flight hours and 30,000 landings. Its two turboprop engines can produce 680-shaft horsepower each, but are derated to 500 to give the T-44A greater economy and longer life. These qualities, along with a Beech-supported service and overhaul program which was part of the purchase agreement, enabled the T-44As to continue their outstanding record for reliability. During their first three years of operation, for example, the T-44As logged more than 86,000 flight hours with an average operational readiness ratio of over 90 percent, a figure which exceeded Navy contract requirements.

SPECIFICATIONS AND PERFORMANCE

Manufacturer: Beech Aircraft Corporation, Wichita, Kansas

Type: Twin-engine advanced training aircraft

Accommodation: Instructor, two students, and two observers

Power plant: Two Pratt & Whitney Aircraft of Canada PT6A-34V turboprop engines of 550 shaft hp (410 kw) each, driving Hartzell 3-blade metal, full-feathering, reversible pitch propellers

Dimensions: Span, 50 ft. 3 in. (15 m); length, 35 ft. 6 in. (10.6 m); height, 14 ft. 2.6 in. (4.27 m)

Weights: Empty, 6,326 lb. (2,869 kg); max. takeoff wgt., 9,650 lb. (4,377 kg); max. landing wgt., 9,168 lb. (4,159 kg)

Performance: Max. cruise speed, 276 mph (444 km/h); rate of climb, 1,960 ft./min. (588 m); service ceiling, 29,500 ft. (8,850 m); stall speed, flaps down, 86 mph (139 km/h); max. range, 1,455 miles (2,340 km)

Armament: None

ROCKWELL INTERNATIONAL T-2 BUCKEYE   The twin-jet T-2C Buckeye has the sleek look of a fighter. Indeed its performance and technical data read more like those of a combat aircraft than a training plane: level flight speeds over 500 miles an hour, a ceiling well above 40,000 feet, and provisions for carrying a variety of guns, bombs, and missiles.

The Naval Air Training Command uses the T-2C for a wide range of jet training, from a student's first jet flight through advance training and fighter tactics. In the Buckeye the fledgling jet flier learns formation and aerobatic flying at high speeds and high altitudes; basic and radio instruments; day and night navigation; gunnery, bombing, and carrier operations.

Twin-jet T-2C Buckeye, with its 500 mph speed, is a jet trainer with combat aircraft performance.

Formation of T-2C Buckeyes shows sleek look of this trainer with features of the latest jet fighters.

The Buckeye's tandem seating arrangement, with the instructor in an elevated rear seat, provides excellent visibility for both pupil and teacher. The cockpits have dual controls, pressurization, and air conditioning. Like the latest jet fighter and attack aircraft, they have ejection seats for emergency escape from ground level to high altitudes and at speeds from 60 to 600 miles an hour.

The T-2C combines the flight qualities needed in a trainer: quick response to the controls, low landing speed, and good stability. In addition, the wide-tread tricycle landing gear provides good control during takeoff and landing, and the airframe is built to withstand the unintentional high "g" loads and rough landings encountered in student training. The plane has an arresting hook for real or simulated carrier landings.

The Buckeye's beginnings date back to 1956 when the Navy drew up requirements for an all-purpose jet trainer. North American Aviation, of Inglewood, California, then producing the T-28 piston engine trainer for Navy basic training, was chosen to develop the new aircraft. To save time and money, many parts and equipment already proven in operation were used in the new trainer; the control system, for example, was similar to that of the T-28C, while the wing design was derived from that of North American's F-J1 Fury jet fighter.

The first version of the Buckeye had a single jet engine (the Westinghouse J34 of 3,400 pounds thrust) and made its initial flight on January 31, 1958. Deliveries to the Training Command started in July of 1959 and eventually reached a total of about 120 aircraft. In 1962 the Columbus Aircraft Division of North American Rockwell (which later became Rockwell International) received a contract to modify the Buckeye as a twin-jet trainer with two Pratt & Whitney J60 engines providing a total thrust of 6,000 pounds. The modified trainer, the T-2B, first flew on August 30, 1962, at Columbus, Ohio, and the Navy purchased almost 100 of the new aircraft.

Another power plant change came in 1968 when twin General Electric J85 engines replaced the J60s, the change leading to the current model, the T-2C, which first took to the air on April 17, 1968. The Navy bought more than 230 of the new model. The A and B models were retired from service in the 1970s, leaving the T-2C to carry on the Buckeye name as the Navy's basic jet trainer into the 1980s.

SPECIFICATIONS AND PERFORMANCE

Manufacturer: Columbus Aircraft Division, Rockwell International Corporation, Columbus, Ohio.

Type: All-purpose jet trainer

Accommodation: Student and instructor seated in tandem

Power plant: Two General Electric J85-GE-4 turbojet engines of 2,950 lb. (1,338 kg) thrust each

Dimensions: Span, 38 ft. 2 in. (11.6 m); length, 38 ft. 8 in. (11.8 m); height, 14 ft. 9 in. (4.5 m); wing area, 255 sq. ft. (23.68 sq. m)

Weights: Empty, 8,115 lb. (3,681 kg); gross wgt., 13,180 lb. (5,978 kg)

Performance: Max. speed, 535 mph (861 km/h); initial climb, 6,200 ft./min. (1,860 m); service ceiling, 45,200 ft. (13,777 m); range, 1,069 miles (1,721 km)

Armament: Two underwing attachment points of 320-lb. (145-kg) capacity each; one .50-cal. gun; bomb racks, rocket packs, and an accessory kit for six more attachment points

NORTH AMERICAN T-28 TROJAN   The T-28 Trojan, the first U.S. primary trainer to have a tricycle landing gear, has seen more than three decades of service and is one of the most widely used training planes in U.S. military history.

Bearing the company designation NA-159, the design won a competition in 1948 for a new trainer which would combine the primary and basic training programs in a single aircraft. The new trainer, designated T-28A, made its flight debut on September 16, 1949.

Except for its tricycle undercarriage, the aircraft was of standard trainer design, with a conventional low wing, tandem seating, and a piston type power plant, the 800-horsepower Wright R-1300 radial engine.

The T-28 was originally developed to meet U.S. Air Force requirements and entered service with the

T-28 Trojans have served as Navy basic trainers for three decades. T-28C models are still in service.

Underside view shows T-28C's clean lines, arresting hook for carrier practice landings.

Air Force Training Command in 1950. Eventually 1,194 T-28As were built for the Air Force.

The Navy introduced the Trojan into its program for new pilots in 1952 following a Department of Defense decision to standardize training methods and equipment between the Air Force and the Navy. The new model, the T-28B, had been developed for the Navy by North American following Navy evaluation of the T-28A. The Navy version had several changes, most notably the installation of a larger power plant, the 1,425-horsepower Wright R-1820-86 engine, which boosted the Trojan's top speed from 285 to 346 miles an hour.

Deliveries of the T-28B totalled 489, some of which were later modified as DT-28Bs for use in the remote control of drone target aircraft. An additional 299 Trojans, delivered to the Navy as T-28Cs, differed only in having arresting gear for use in simulated carrier landings on airfields and also aboard carriers. The T-28B has been retired from service but the T-28C remains in operation at the Pensacola, Florida, and Kingsville, Texas, Naval Air Stations.

Manufacturer: North American Aviation, Inc., Inglewood, California

Type: Basic trainer

Accommodation: Student and instructor in tandem

Power plant: One Wright R-1820-56S piston engine of 1,425 hp

Dimensions: Span, 40 ft. 7 in. (12.18 m); length, 34 ft. 4 in. (10.29 m); height, 12 ft. 8 in. (3.78 m); wing area, 271 sq. ft. (25.2 sq. m)

Weights: Empty, 6,512 lb. (2,954 kg); normal gross wgt., 8,118 lb. (3,682 kg); max. landing wgt., 8,495 lb. (3,853 kg)

Performance: Max. speed, 346 mph (557 km/h); cruise speed, 310 mph (499 km/h); initial climb, 3,540 ft./min. (1,062 m); service ceiling, 35,000 ft. (10,500 m); range, 1,060 miles (1,705 km)

Armament: Accessory kits providing for bombs, rockets, and machine guns

NORTH AMERICAN T-39 SABRELINER   The twin-jet T-39 is a multipurpose military version of the civilian Sabreliner, which is known chiefly as a high-speed executive transport.

With its cruise speed of 500 miles an hour at 40,000 feet (above most weather), the T-39 matches

North American T-39 Sabreliner's chief training use is for instruction of radar operators.

today's jet airliners in performance. The Sabreliner's swept-back wing, leading edge slats, and tail assembly give it a strong resemblance to the North American F-86 Sabre (the first sweptwing U.S. fighter) and the F-100 Super Sabre. In size and weight, the Sabreliner falls roughly between those two history-making fighters.

The basic configuration of the T-39 provides for a crew of two and four passengers. The cabin can be changed from a radar or navigation trainer arrangement to that of a cargo or passenger carrier in a matter of minutes. As a cargo transport the Sabreliner can carry items weighing up to 2,300 pounds with a length of 16 feet. Tie-down fittings for the removable passenger seats can also be used as cargo rings in lashing down equipment.

The prototype Sabreliner rolled from North American's assembly line May 9, 1958. The Navy selected the T-39 in 1962 as a trainer for maritime radar operators. First designated T3J-1 and later T-39D, the Navy Sabreliner carried Magnavox radar systems and was powered by two turbojet engines attached to either side of the aft fuselage. Deliveries to the Naval Air Training Command at Pensacola, Florida, began in August, 1963. The 42 Sabreliners built for the Navy have been used chiefly in the training of nonflying officers. Training versions of the Sabreliner are also used by the U.S. Air Force.

SPECIFICATIONS AND PERFORMANCE

Manufacturer: North American Aviation, Inc., Inglewood, California

Type: Twin-jet trainer for nonflying officers; secondary mission, VIP and cargo transport

Accommodation: Pilot, copilot; seats for four students or passengers

Power plant: Two Pratt & Whitney J60-P-3A turbojet engines of 3,000 lb. (1,368 kg) thrust each

Dimensions: Span, 44 ft. 6 in. (13.35 m); length, 44 ft. (13.2 m); height, 16 ft. (4.8 m); wing area, 342.1 sq. ft. (31.78 sq. m)

Weights: Empty, 9,265 lb. (4,203 kg); max. gross takeoff wgt., 17,760 lb. (8,056 kg)

Performance: Max. speed, 550 mph (884.9 km/h); cruise speed, 500 mph (804.4 km/h); cruise altitude, above 40,000 ft. (12,000 m); cruise range, 1,950 miles (3,137.5 km); takeoff run, 2,500 ft. (750 m); landing run, 1,850 ft. (555 m); landing speed, 113 mph (181.8 km/h)

Armament: None

VOUGHT TA-7C CORSAIR II The TA-7C Corsair II is a two-place aircraft converted from earlier model Navy A-7 attack planes and designed as a combat crew trainer and instrument trainer. It is carrier-suitable and could easily be adapted for combat operations either from aircraft carriers or shore bases.

After a prototype, the YA-7H, had made hundreds of test flights to prove the feasibility of the conversion, Vought Corporation began the remanufacture of 65 of the earlier model A-7s into the TA-7Cs. The first production TA-7C was test flown on December 17, 1976, and delivered to the Navy on January 31, 1977. Deliveries continued into 1980.

The TA-7C two-seater retains most of the physical qualities of the single-seat A-7. It is 34 inches (86.4 centimeters) longer and four inches (10.2 centimeters) higher at the tail. The added length consists of a new 16-inch section in the forward part of the fuselage and about 18 inches at the trailing edge of the wing.

Tandem-seat Vought TA-7C was converted as a combat and instrument trainer from the A-7E Corsair II.

TA-7C trainer (top) is 34 inches longer than the A-7E (foreground), but retains most of the features of the attack aircraft. Note redesign of cockpit.

The aft fuselage was modified by an upward slant of a little over one degree, thus permitting approach and landing attitudes identical with those of the A-7E attack aircraft in spite of the longer fuselage. The rear seat is elevated to provide exceptional visibility for the instructor/pilot.

The wing and fuselage weapons attachment points are retained and a 20-mm Gatling gun, with 500 rounds of ammunition, provides weapons system training. The TA-7C has the same computerized navigation and weapon delivery system as the A-7E. Despite the addition of the second cockpit, the TA-7C retains all the internal fuel capacity (about 1,500 gallons) of the A-7E, giving it unusually long range without external tanks. The TA-7C also has the aerial refueling capability of the A-7E.

One side-opening canopy covers both cockpits. Each cockpit has all controls, communications, navigation equipment, and displays required for airplane and related systems instruction. A closed-circuit television system provides the instructor with the same displays seen by the student in the front seat.

Powered by one turbofan jet engine, the TA-7C has the same performance as other Corsair II aircraft. A parabrake is installed for short field landings.

As a trainer, the two-place A-7 permits instructor/pilots to ride with their students instead of flying formation in another aircraft, thus providing improved training with fewer aircraft. The savings in the reduced number of aircraft needed, including lower operating, support, and manpower costs, amount to several million dollars per year at the U.S. Navy carrier replacement air wing training facilities at Cecil Field, Florida, and Lemoore, California.

SPECIFICATIONS AND PERFORMANCE

Manufacturer: Vought Corporation, a subsidiary of LTV Corporation, Dallas, Texas

Type: Combat crew and instrument trainer

Accommodation: Student/pilot and instructor/pilot in tandem

Power plant: One Pratt & Whitney TF30-P-8 turbofan engine of 12,200 lb. (5,534 kg) thrust

Dimensions: Span, 38 ft. 9 in. (11.8 m); length, 48 ft. 8 in. (14.8 m); height, 16 ft. 4 in. (4.79 m)

Weights: Empty, 19,180 lb. (8,700 kg); takeoff wgt., 31,982 lb. (14,540 kg)

Performance: Max. speed, 669 mph (1,077 km/h); takeoff run, 4,030 ft. (1,228 m); landing run, 3,000 ft. (914 m); radius of action, 791 miles (1,273 km); ferry range, internal fuel, 2,265 miles (3,645 km)

Armament: Provisions for carrying weapons available for A-7E Corsair II including one 20-mm multi-barrel gun, various combinations of missiles, and bombs up to 15,000 lb. (6,805 kg)

Gear down, and slots and flaps extended, a TA-7C makes an approach for a practice landing.

DOUGLAS TA-4 SKYHAWK   The TA-4F is a two-place advanced trainer version of the single-seat Douglas A-4 Skyhawk, the lightweight attack aircraft previously described.

In 1964, after ten years of Skyhawk production, covering five different attack versions, Douglas made design studies of single-seat and two-seat models of the Skyhawk for export. The Navy ordered the two-seat TA-4E advanced trainer version that year.

The two cockpits in tandem necessitated a slightly longer fuselage, and the second cockpit restricted the size of the fuel tank in the fuselage. All the other operational features of the A-4E attack version were retained, including the Pratt & Whitney J52 turbojet engine.

The two prototype TA-4Es first flew on June 30 and August 2, 1965, respectively, and the new trainer entered production as the TA-4F in April, 1966. The first TA-4F was delivered to the Naval Air Station, Lemoore, California, on May 19, 1966, with production eventually reaching a total of 238 aircraft.

These were followed from mid-1969 onwards by more than 200 TA-4Js, a simplified version of the TA-4F with much nonessential equipment deleted. Despite the deletions, provisions remained for installing, among others, such items as radar, a low-altitude bombing system, air-to-ground missile systems, a gun pod, and an in-flight refueling system. (For general design and structures information on the TA-4F see the Douglas A-4 Skyhawk in the Attack Aircraft section.)

SPECIFICATIONS AND PERFORMANCE (TA-4F)

Manufacturer: Douglas Aircraft Company, Long Beach, California

Type: Turbojet-powered advanced trainer

Accommodation: Student/pilot and instructor/pilot

Power plant: One Pratt & Whitney J52-P-8A turbojet engine of 9,300 lb. (4,218 kg) thrust

Dimensions: Span, 27 ft. 6 in. (8.38 m); length, 42 ft. 7¼ in. (12.98 m); height, 15 ft. 3 in. (4.66 m); wing area, 260 sq. ft. (24.16 sq. m)

Weights: Empty, 10,700 lb. (4,853 kg); normal takeoff wgt., 24,500 lb. (11,113 kg)

Performance: Max. speed, 654 mph (1,052 km/h); max. rate of climb (approx.), 8,000 ft./min. (2,440 m); takeoff run (approx.), 3,000 ft. (1,000 m); max. ferry range (approx.), 2,000 miles (3,225 km)

Armament: Full range of weapons available for A-4 Skyhawk, including two 20-mm guns in wings, and up to 9,155 lb. (4,153 kg) of bombs, missiles, rockets, and fuel tanks on five attachment points under wings and fuselage

Douglas TA-4F jet-powered advanced trainer retains the performance and combat capabilities of the A-4F Skyhawk.

Bell TH-57A, a three-place primary training helicopter, is a military version of the Bell 206A Jet Ranger, most widely used turbine helicopter in the world.

BELL TH-57A SEA RANGER

The TH-57A is a military version of the world's most widely used commercial turbine-powered helicopter, the Bell model 206A Jet Ranger.

The Navy ordered 40 of the dual-control TH-57As in 1968 as its primary light turbine-training helicopter for operation at the Naval Air Station, Pensacola, Florida. It was a virtual "off-the-shelf" purchase, the aircraft differing little from the civilian model.

With good flight stability, rapid response to the controls, and high maneuverability at any speed, the Sea Ranger has provided an ideal introduction to rotary-winged aircraft. The principals of helicopter flight proved to be simple to teach and easy to learn in the TH-57A.

The Sea Ranger is a sister craft to the U.S. Army's OH-58C Kiowa, a light observation helicopter, another derivative of the Bell 206A.

Manufacturer: Bell Helicopter Textron, a division of Textron, Inc., Fort Worth, Texas

Type: Turbine-powered primary training helicopter

Accommodation: Student and instructor, seated side-by-side; one observer

Power plant: One Allison 250-C-18 turbine engine of 317 max. shaft hp (for 5 minutes), 270 shaft hp (for continuous operation)

Dimensions: Rotor diameter, 33 ft. 4 in. (9.9 m); length, 38 ft. 9 in. (11.6 m)

Weights: Empty (approx.), 1,900 lb. (862 kg); mission wgt., 2,558 lb. (1,160 kg); max. gross wgt., 2,900 lb. (1,315 kg)

Performance: Max. speed, 149.5 mph (240.5 km/h); max. rate of climb, 1,030 ft./min. (310 m); service ceiling, 16,200 ft. (4,860 m); max. range, 260 miles (579 km)

Armament: None

BELL TH-1L IROQUOIS　　Another Bell aircraft used in the Navy's training program is the TH-1L for advanced helicopter pilot instruction.

　　The TH-1L is a single-engine Iroquois type, similar to the U.S. Army Huey and the Marine Corps UH-1E (see Bell UH-1 Iroquois in Part Seven/Transport) but fitted with special equipment for the training role.

Bell TH-1L Iroquois advanced trainer was adapted from the Army's Huey troop transport.

The first of 90 TH-1Ls was delivered to the Naval Air Station, Pensacola, Florida, in November, 1969, with deliveries continuing through 1970. The Navy's UH-1L utility and HH-1K rescue helicopters are also similar to the TH-1L and were built during the same period of 1969–70.

SPECIFICATIONS AND PERFORMANCE

Manufacturer: Bell Helicopter Textron, a division of Textron, Inc., Fort Worth, Texas

Type: Turbine-powered advanced training helicopter

Accommodation: Student and instructor; several observers

Power plant: One Lycoming T53-L-13 turboshaft engine of 1,100 shaft hp

Dimensions: Main rotor diameter, 48 ft. 3 in. (14.5 m); tail rotor diameter, 8 ft. 6 in. (2.5 m); length, 40 ft. 8 in. (12 m); height, 13 ft. 7 in. (4 m)

Weights: Empty, 4,800 lb. (2,177 kg); gross wgt., 9,500 lb. (4,309 kg)

Performance: Max. speed, 126 mph (202 km/h); cruise speed, 106 mph (170 km/h); service ceiling, 12,600 ft. (3,780 m); rate of climb, 1,630 ft./min. (489 m)

Armament: None

GRUMMAN TE-2C HAWKEYE

The TE-2C trainer version of the Hawkeye deserves only a footnote in this listing of today's Naval aircraft, since only two were ever flown.

Grumman did not actually produce a trainer model of the E-2C. Rather, at the Navy's request, the company modified two E-2Cs into two TE-2Cs. The changes consisted of removing the radar equipment from inside the aircraft and substituting lead weights to maintain the aircraft's balance. The two TE-2Cs are now operating at the Naval Air Station, Norfolk, Virginia, as part of an East Coast Training Squadron.

Externally, there is no difference between the TE-2C and the E-2C Hawkeye described in Part Four/Reconnaissance Aircraft. Specifications and performance data are also essentially the same.

Two Bell TH-1Ls circle an aircraft carrier during advanced helicopter training flight.

Part Ten / THE FUTURE

What does the future hold for U.S. Naval Aviation? What problems confront it and how ready will it be to carry out its responsibilities in a world beset by the constant threat of war? Can our fleet control oceans patrolled by a potential enemy's growing force of missile-firing submarines, ships, and aircraft?

The good news is that U.S. Naval Aviation has never been more impressive in peacetime, especially in the quality of its technology and equipment and the professionalism of its people. The aircraft which we have seen in the previous pages—both those that have been updated and improved over the years and the new ones soon to enter service—provide the best evidence of high quality.

The bad news is that, for the near future at least, the approved purchases of new aircraft fall far below what is needed to replace the machines which are lost each year to obsolescence and the occasional inevitable accidents. For the past eight or nine years there has been insufficient money approved to buy as many aircraft as were lost. However, with the change in the Administration in 1981 there appears to be a change in policy which may turn the situation around.

It is bad news also that Naval Aviation, because of its low pay scales, loses too many experienced people each year to business and industry. As a result, all signs show a dangerous shortage of pilots and supporting ground crews. The shortages have especially hit the mid-officer and mid-enlisted ranks—the senior lieutenants and junior lieutenant-commanders, and the senior and junior petty officers. Many of the petty officers had 8 to 12 years of experience and, with an emphasis on management training, assumed much responsibility early in their careers.

To help meet the problems of equipment shortages the Navy will stick to its course of extending the service life of certain aircraft and modernizing others. Bright spots in the picture are the continued receipt of four outstanding airplane types—the F-14 Tomcat fighter, including several for use as high-speed reconnaissance planes; the P-C3 Orion long-range patrol plane; the E-2C Hawkeye early warning aircraft; and the EA-6B Prowler with its unprecedented array of electronic jamming equipment. The Navy refers to the Prowler as being "among the more important production programs" and "the only tactical ECM (Electronic Countermeasures) aircraft currently in production."

Diagrams of F/A-18A Hornet show outlines of single-seat, twin-jet, twin-mission strike fighter designed to serve into the twenty-first century.

F/A-18A

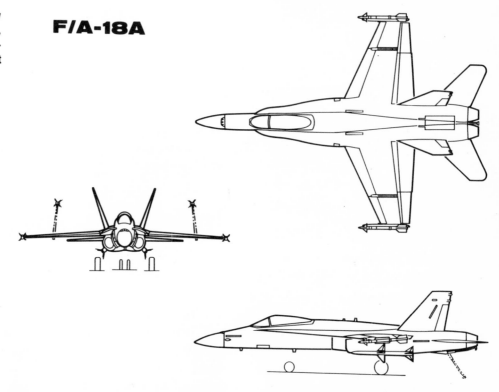

Further brightening the airplane outlook are the imminent deliveries of the high-performance F-18 Hornet, more recently referred to as the F/A-18, since it is to be flown as an attack as well as a fighter aircraft. This use of a single (or common) airframe for both missions is an efficient, cost-saving plan because it is necessary to train only one, rather than two, maintenance crews, to handle both fighter and attack versions.

The two new helicopters—the SH-60B Seahawk (for use in LAMPS Mark III) and the CH-53E Super

SH-60B Seahawk helicopter deploys a Magnetic Anomaly Detector (MAD), one of several antisubmarine devices used in Navy's new Light Airborne Multi-Purpose System (LAMPS).

Stallion—are also expected to play key roles in the future. LAMPS III, according to the report of the Chief of Naval Operations for fiscal year 1981, "is essential as an effective counter to the increasing threat of Soviet missiles and torpedoes—both surface- and subsurface-launched." As we saw earlier, LAMPS III is a fully-integrated ship/helicopter system whose primary mission is antisubmarine warfare with a secondary task of antiship surveillance and targeting. The ponderous Super Stallion, with its three turbines and 16-ton lift, will probably grow in importance as the fleet's heavy hauler of supplies from shore-to-ship and ship-to-ship and, with the Marines, as an assault transport operating from the decks of special helicopter carriers. Another Navy use of the Super Stallion might be mine countermeasures—the towing of a new generation of sleds and equipment which will be larger and heavier than today's and would require the added power of larger copters.

To help solve its manpower problems the Navy has been expanding its recruiting efforts emphasizing

Next generation of helicopter minesweepers will be a variant of CH-53E Super Stallion, the MH-53E, shown here in drawing by artist Andy Whyte.

better leadership through a management education program, improving working conditions ashore and at sea, and seeking to revitalize the Naval Reserve as a strong and effective organization. Its continuing requests for pay increases, especially in such specialized areas as aviation, submarines, and sea duty, have won increasing Congressional support the past year. A 16 percent pay raise as of October, 1980, and other increases proposed for the near future, may eventually stop the flow of people out of Naval Aviation.

The job facing Naval Aviation reflects the magnitude of the task confronting the Navy as a whole. "The Navy's Plight: Too Many Seas to Cover," asserted a headline over a military analysis in *The New York Times*. "U.S. Officials Worried by New Soviet Sub," said a *Washington Post* headline. (The vessel referred to is a new attack submarine, code-named Oscar, which, Navy officials said, "Will extend the lethal reach of Soviet anticarrier forces from today's 20 miles to 200 miles.")

The latest edition of the authoritative *Jane's Fighting Ships* is, in the words of one columnist, "for the first time, gloomy" about U.S. Naval strength. America's two-ocean navy, *Jane's* says, has "a potential in both the Atlantic and Pacific of six carriers, about 40 submarines, 12 cruisers, 50 super destroyers, and 34 frigates." This represents a total of 12 carrier battle groups. (A carrier battle group consists of missile-firing surface vessels and attack submarines built around an aircraft carrier.)

The problem with a two-ocean Navy, as another analyst points out, is that the Navy has a third ocean to cover, the Indian, plus the Mediterranean Sea, and the Navy believes it needs "a minimum of 15 carrier battle groups in a Navy of about 590 ships" to cover the "three-and-a-half oceans" involved. At the moment the Navy has forces which senior officers feel are "barely adequate for a one-and-a-half ocean fleet," the analyst said. This line of thinking seems not to be falling on deaf ears, for the new Administration has plans to increase Naval strength to the 15 carrier battle groups.

A recent official report from the Chief of Naval Operations (for fiscal year 1981) casts further light on the problems. "The total number of ships in the U.S. fleet," said the report, "has declined significantly and steadily since the mid-1960s, down from over 1,000 to 540 today."

The report noted that, "With respect to the Soviet fleet the U.S. Navy is outnumbered by more than three-to-one overall. Although we dominate in aircraft carriers, the Soviet navy has 80 more principal surface fighting ships, 235 more submarines, six times as many auxiliaries, and a land-based aviation

Silhouetted against a setting sun, F-14 Tomcat is symbolic of U.S. Naval power of today and tomorrow.

strike force. Furthermore, in quality—a traditional area of advantage for the United States—Soviet naval forces are narrowing the U.S. lead year by year."

A comparison of the total number of vessels in the active fleets for the years 1969 and 1979, as disclosed in the report, are: U.S., down from 926 vessels to 462; Soviets, up from 1,670 vessels to 1,764. Finally, the report stated that the U.S. Navy's 12 carrier battle groups with their tactical air wings represent the bare minimum necessary for retaining a credible offensive capability.

"Given current Soviet force levels," the report declared, "a U.S. Navy force structure of at least 550 ships, of the proper mix and capability, is needed to ensure the United States maintains maritime superiority. This requires that, over the long term, about 18 new ships per year be procured to modernize the fleet at an acceptable rate and maintain current force levels."

Such a force would require regular purchase of new aircraft, including many of the high-performance airplanes and helicopters covered in this book. Given these aircraft and sufficient crews to fly and maintain them, Naval Aviation, on the evidence of history, can be counted on to carry on its traditions of achievement. In this way Naval Aviation would continue its unique contributions to our national strength, with the ultimate aim of advancing the cause of world peace by discouraging any potential aggressor.

This ultimate goal is all-important because the threat to our nation's security may be looked upon as two-fold: 1—Nuclear blackmail, in which we could be denied such a primary source of energy as petroleum, along with such vital strategic materials as titanium, cobalt, nickel, and tungsten; 2—Nuclear war itself, which would level whole cities, incinerating millions of people instantly and making the earth uninhabitable. Under such threats, the deterrent effect of military power may be mankind's best hope for survival—at least until all nations truly understand that nuclear war would be a "no-win" catastrophe for all concerned.

INDEX

Aeronautical Engine Laboratory, 15
AFCS (automatic flight control system, 104, 107
Airborne Early Warning (AEW), 61, 134
Aircraft carriers, 16–17, 19, 21, 26, 28–29, 35, 39, 42, 50, 54, 127, 139
Allison engines, 51, 62, 64, 88, 92, 98, 131
America (flying boat), 16
Antarctic operations, 35, 95–98, 102, 104
Armstrong, William J., 11
ASW (antisubmarine warfare), 34, 35, 73, 75, 76, 77, 78, 82, 86, 87, 93, 136
Attack aircraft, 48–57

Battle of Midway Island, 25
Battle of the Coral Sea, 25
Beechcraft King Air (T-44A), 116–117
Beechcraft Mentor (T-34), 114–115
Beechcraft Super King Air, 89, 90
Beechcraft UC-12B, 89–90
Bell Iroquois (HH-1K), 113
Bell Iroquois (TH-1L), 131–133
Bell Iroquois (UH-1), 102–104, 113, 131
Bell Jet Ranger (206A), 130
Bell Sea Ranger (TH-57A), 130–131
Birmingham (cruiser), 11–12
Blimps, 11, 15, 28
Boeing F4B, 17, 18
Boeing Vertol Sea Knight (H-46), 36, 98–101, 112

Boeing Vertol Sea Knight (HH-46), 112
Boyington, Major Gregory, 28–29
Brow, Lieutenant Harold, 17
Burgess Company, 10

Catapult launching, 14, 17, 21, 41, 42
Chambers, Captain Washington Irving, 11, 12, 13
Chevalier, Lieutenant Godfrey deC., 14
Cochran, Jacqueline, 72
COD (carrier-on-board delivery) planes, 91, 93
Consolidated Catalina (PBY), 22, 24
Consolidated Coronado (PB2Y), 22, 25
Cuban crisis, 68
Curtiss A-3 (hydroplane), 13
Curtiss AB-3, 14
Curtiss flying boats, 10, 14, 15, 16
Curtiss, Glenn H., 12, 16
Curtiss Helldiver (SB2C), 22
Curtiss N-9 (trainer), 14
Curtiss NC-4 (flying boat), 16
Curtiss Seagull (SOC), 22
Curtiss Triad (A-1), 13

Dirigibles, 10, 11, 17, 20
Douglas Dauntless (SBD), 22
Douglas DC-3, 105
Douglas Devastator (TBD), 22
Douglas Skyhawk (A-4), 36, 49, 56–57, 128
Douglas Skyhawk (TA-4), 128, 129
Douglas Skyraider, 33

Douglas Skywarrior (A-3D), 36, 54–55
Douglas torpedo planes, 19

ECM (electronic countermeasures), 59, 71, 134
Edwards AFB, 68, 72
Ellyson, Lieutenant Theodore G., 12
Ely, Eugene, 11, 12, 16
Erickson, Commander Frank, 110
ESM (electronic support measures) system, 75, 84, 93

Fastest transport, 105
Fighter aircraft, 37–47
First Navy airplane, 13
First sweptwing fighter, 124
First turbine primary trainer, 114, 115
Fleet Air Reconnaissance Squadrons, 63
Fleet Tactical Support Squadron, 91
FLIR (forward-looking infrared) scanner, 75
Flying boats, 15, 16, 19, 31

General Dynamics YF-16, 44
General Electric engines, 43, 47, 67, 72, 76, 78, 82, 85, 101, 109, 120
Grumman Avenger (TBF), 22, 27
Grumman F2F-1, 22
Grumman Greyhound (C-2A), 91–92
Grumman Hawkeye (E-2C), 36, 60, 61, 62, 134
Grumman Hawkeye (TE-2C), 133
Grumman Hellcat (F6F), 22, 29

Grumman Intruder (A-6E), 51–53, 58
Grumman Panther (F9F-2), first Navy production jet, 33, 34
Grumman Prowler (EA-6B), 36, 58–59, 134
Grumman Tomcat (F-14), 36, 37–39, 134
Grumman Tracker (S-2), 75, 93
Grumman Trader (C-1A), 93–94
Grumman Wildcat (F4F), 22, 23

Hamilton Standard propellers, 62, 88, 92
Hartzell propellers, 115, 117
Helicopters, 2, 11, 31, 34, 65–67, 76–79, 80–82, 83–85, 98–101, 102–104, 107–109, 110–113, 130–133, 135, 136
Herreshoff, Captain Nathanael, 9, 10

Isherwood system, 9

Jet fighters, first appearance of, 33, 34

Kaman Seasprite (HH-2), 110, 111
Kaman Seasprite (SH-2), 80–82
Kawasaki Heavy Industries, Inc., 99
Korean conflict, 33, 34

LAMPS (Light Airborne Multi-Purpose System), 82, 83, 84, 110, 135, 136
Langley (first aircraft carrier), 19
Largest helicopter, 107
Lockheed Constellation (EC-121), 35, 88
Lockheed Hercules (C-130), 95–98
Lockheed Hercules (EC-130Q), 63–64

Lockheed Neptune (P2V), 30, 31, 32, 73, 86
Lockheed Orion (P-3), 36, 73, 86–88, 134
Lockheed Viking (S-3A), 73–76
Los Angeles (dirigible), 20
Lycoming engines, 113, 133

MAD (magnetic anomaly detector), 75, 84, 86, 136
Martin Mariner (PBM), 22, 25
Martin Marlin (P5M), 31
Martin Seamaster (P6M), jet flying boat, 31, 32, 33
Martin torpedo planes, 19
McDonnell Douglas Hornet (F-18), 44–47, 50, 135
McDonnell Douglas Phantom II (F-4), 36, 40–43
McDonnell Douglas Skytrain II (C-9B), 105–107
MCM (mine countermeasures) squadrons, 65, 67
Minesweeping, 65, 66, 67, 77, 136
Mustin, Lieutenant-Commander Henry C., 13

National Science Foundation, 95
Naval Air Stations, 18, 21, 39, 55, 68, 75, 80, 89, 114, 117, 122, 128, 133
Naval Air Systems Command, 11
Naval Air Test Center, 55, 63, 88, 97, 109
Naval Air Training Command, 116, 118, 124
Naval Aircraft Factory, 16
NC-4 (flying boat), 10, 17

North American Sabreliner (T-39), 123–124
North American Trojan (T-28), 121–123
North American Vigilante (RA-5C), 70–72
North Carolina (cruiser), 14
North Island, San Diego, 12
Northrop YF-17, 44–45, 47
NWDS (Navigation/Weapons Delivery System), 50

O'Hare, Lieutenant Edward, 28, 29
Operation Deep Freeze, 35, 95–98, 102, 104
Operation High Jump, 35

Patrol aircraft, 86–88
Pearl Harbor, 23, 24
Pennsylvania (cruiser), 12
Pensacola, first Naval Air Station, 13, 14
Phoenix missile, 38
Polaris missile, 31, 36
Poseidon missile, 36
Pratt & Whitney engines, 17, 39, 53, 56, 57, 59, 70, 107, 120, 124, 127, 128

Radial air-cooled engine, 16, 121
Radome, 61, 86, 88, 93
Read, Lieutenant-Commander Albert C., 16
Reconnaissance aircraft, 58–72
Rescue aircraft, 110–113
Richardson, Holden C., 13
Rockwell International Buckeye (T-2), 118–120

Rolls Royce engine, 51
Roosevelt, Theodore, 11

Sapphire engine, 57
Schoech, Rear Admiral William A., 72
Search aircraft, 73–85
Sikorsky Sea King (HH-3A), 110, 111, 112
Sikorsky Sea King (SH-3), 36, 76–78, 79, 111
Sikorsky Sea Stallion (RH-53D), 36, 65–67
Sikorsky Seahawk (SH-60B), 83–85, 135, 136
Sikorsky Super Stallion (CH-53E), 107–109, 135, 136, 137
Space programs, Naval Aviation's part in, 35–36, 78, 79
Stearman N2S-3 ("Yellow Peril"), 24
Submarines, 10, 33, 36, 75, 98

TACAMO squadrons, 64
Towers, Lieutenant John J., 13

Trainer aircraft, 114–133
TRAM (Target Recognition Attack Multisensor), 51, 52
Transport aircraft, 89–109
Trident missile, 36
Twin-jet trainer, 118, 119, 120
TwinPac power plant, 104

United Aircraft of Canada (Pratt & Whitney) engines, 90, 104, 115, 117
U.S. Air Force, 40, 42, 90, 97, 114, 121, 124
U.S. Army, 84, 90, 130, 131
U.S. Marine Corps, 15, 16, 17, 28, 34, 40, 42, 44, 47, 56, 59, 68, 90, 97, 98, 100, 101, 102, 104, 107, 109, 136
U.S. Naval Aviation: current aircraft, 37–133; future, 134–140; Golden Year, 35; historic ties to ships, 9–10; history, 11–36; two-ocean Navy, 20, 26, 138
U.S. Navy air records and awards, 17, 31, 41–42, 64, 68

Verne, Jules, 9
Vertical replenishment, 101
Vietnam War, 52, 61, 65, 78, 81, 113
Viner, Dmitri, 110
Vought Corsair (F4U), 22, 29, 33
Vought Corsair (O2U-1), 21
Vought Corsair II (A-7E), 36, 48–51, 52
Vought Corsair II (TA-7C), 125–127
Vought Crusader (RF-8G), 36, 68–69
Vought Kingfisher (OS2U), 22, 30
Vought VE-7, 19
Vought Vindicator (SB2U), 22

Westinghouse engines, 55, 120
Williams, Lieutenant Al, 17
Windsor, Commander R. W., 68
"Wingless" flights, 69–70
World War I, 15–16
World War II, 16, 22, 26–29, 34, 54, 73
Wright engines, 57, 84, 123

"Yellow Peril" trainer, 24